MW00579687

Afflicting the Comfortable,
Comforting the Afflicted

Afflicting the Comfortable, *Comforting the Afflicted*

A Guide to Law and Gospel Preaching

Glenn L. Monson

Foreword by
Craig Alan Satterlee

WIPF & STOCK · Eugene, Oregon

AFFLICTING THE COMFORTABLE,
COMFORTING THE AFFLICTED
A Guide to Law and Gospel Preaching

Copyright © 2015 Glenn L. Monson. All rights reserved. Except for brief
quotations in critical publications or reviews, no part of this book may
be reproduced in any manner without prior written permission from the
publisher. Write: Permissions, Wipf and Stock Publishers, 199 W. 8th Ave.,
Suite 3, Eugene, OR 97401.

Wipf & Stock
An Imprint of Wipf and Stock Publishers
199 W. 8th Ave., Suite 3
Eugene, OR 97401

www.wipfandstock.com

ISBN 13: 978-1-4982-0246-6

Manufactured in the U.S.A.

Biblical citations are from New Revised Standard Version Bible, copyright
1989, Division of Christian Education of the National Council of the
Churches of Christ in the United States of America. Used by permission.
All rights reserved.

References (in text and diagrams) to the Crossings Method are used with
permission of the Crossings Community, Inc., Chesterfield, MO, www.
crossings.org.

Dedicated to my dad
Who first preached God's word to me

Contents

Foreword

SOME SERMONS I HEAR bring to mind an hourglass lying on its side. In the first chamber of the hourglass, we get six or seven minutes of how bad we are, how bad things are, or how bad the world is. Then, in the narrow part of the hourglass, we get a minute or two about Jesus. Finally, in the second chamber of the hourglass, we get six or seven minutes of what we should, ought, and must do.

Other sermons are pep talks. They offer up a vivid description of the sorry state of our lives and the world and what we need to do about it. Then, for inspiration, we get a sentence or two about Jesus freeing and calling us to do what needs to be done.

Still other sermons remind me of Billy Joel—God loves you just the way you are! I frequently find myself thinking that God loves us in spite of the way we are. And God wants more for and from us.

Then there are sermons that send me running to the Lord's table and from the table into the world as a disciple. These sermons make me feel my need of God's grace and freely offer me that grace in such a way that I want to participate in Christ's work of reconciling the world to God by living in a more Christ-like manner. More than hearing about Jesus, Jesus has encountered me in and through the preacher's words. This is what I pray to preach and even more earnestly pray to hear.

Glenn Monson writes for everyone eager for preachers to lay aside hourglasses, pep talks, and love songs in favor of encounters with the living Christ. Dr. Monson describes himself as a "diehard

Lutheran." Lutheran Christians understand themselves, Scripture, and the world in terms of law and gospel. For Glenn, law is encapsulated in the declaration "You need Christ!" and gospel in the proclamation "Here is Christ!" Understanding that judgment and forgiveness are no longer the chief concern of many churchgoers, he successfully expands the law and gospel paradigm—the ways we need Christ and the ways Christ meets our need—to embrace the principal concerns of our lives.

Yet, the key for unlocking this guide for preachers is neither law nor gospel. The key to unlocking this preaching guide is the word *and*. To ensure that both law *and* gospel find their appropriate place in the sermon in ways that speak to both head *and* heart, Glenn brings together Lutheran theologians and the pioneers of the New Homiletic, theory *and* practice, so that preaching is theologically rich *and* immediately relevant. The gift of this book is not as much new information as the way a faithful, experienced preacher integrates theological *and* homiletic insight into a road map that preachers can easily follow to a destination their hearers will appreciate.

This book is biblically rich, overflowing with examples of exegesis and sermons from lectionary texts. The insights are worth the read for both preachers and lovers of scripture. Yet, more than a commentary, we have the opportunity to slip into this preacher's study and watch over his shoulder as he works. Glenn takes us from studying the text to designing the sermon to writing the manuscript to preaching law and gospel. As a teacher of preaching turned bishop, I find that interviewing pastors about their method of sermon preparation and delivery, rather than teaching them mine, is a mutually enriching experience. Spending an afternoon with Glenn Monson via this book, interviewing him about his way of preaching, you will come away enriched, eager for the pulpit, and blessed.

Rev. Craig Alan Satterlee, PhD

Acknowledgments

IT'S HARD TO KNOW where to start when acknowledging one's growth as a preacher. I could begin with my dad, I suppose, who preached the first sermons I ever heard. I well remember making paper airplanes with the bulletins while sitting in the front pew below the pulpit. The fact is, however, I never really thought much about preaching until I was at seminary, so that's where my real formation began.

My preaching teachers at Luther Northwestern Theological Seminary in St. Paul, Minnesota, were all very helpful to me: Sheldon Tostengaard, Michael Rogness, Gracia Grindal, Cathy Malotky, and others. Other faculty who preached regularly in seminary chapel also surely were part of my formation.

When I began my work in the parish, the members of the congregations I served were my teachers. First at St. John's Lutheran Church of Williams Township in Easton, Pennsylvania, and then at Our Savior's Lutheran Church in Austin, Minnesota, the members of these churches graciously listened and occasionally offered their critique as I went through the necessary growing pains of becoming a preacher of God's word. My colleagues at Our Savior's, Pastors Don Deines, Dan Kahl, and Karen Behling, were also valuable partners in my development as a preacher.

Some of my most intense development as a preacher was undoubtedly during my DMin work at the Lutheran School of Theology at Chicago with Richard Jensen and Craig Satterlee. Both of these fine teachers, as well as the innumerable adjunct faculty who graced us with their presence during our time of study, were very important in my study and maturity.

Finally, my wife, Ruth, and our daughters, Abby and Catherine, have been treasured partners and listeners in this journey. They have heard (endured?) more of my sermons than anyone ought to and have done it with good humor and graciousness. Ruth, particularly, has been a great supporter of mine, and it is she who has kept me going during some of my despondent times.

Preaching is never done in isolation. We are, after all, members of the Body of Christ, and together we speak and listen as the Word comes to us. Thank you to all who have encouraged me in this journey.

Introduction

THIS BOOK, *AFFLICTING THE Comfortable, Comforting the Afflicted: A Guide to Law and Gospel Preaching*, has arisen out of one simple need: the need to understand how one might go about preaching a theologically substantive Law and Gospel sermon, *not* in the old-fashioned sense (theologically and biblically correct but not engaging to the listener) but in a way that draws the listener in, doing the work that the law and the gospel are meant to do in the minds and hearts of God's people.

When I was a seminary student at Luther Northwestern Theological Seminary in St. Paul, Minnesota, in the 1980s, we students were presented (quite unintentionally, I believe) with a quandary in regards to our future life as preachers. Without a doubt we received excellent and extensive teaching in biblical exegesis, systematic theology, and Lutheran history and doctrine. We were given the tools to unearth the treasures of any text and understand what was at stake theologically in our preaching, teaching, and practices of pastoral care. Our *foundations* as preachers of God's word were strong. But when it came time to integrate all this knowledge and bring it to bear *in the pulpit*, well, I hate to say it, but we were pretty much on our own. I puzzled at this. We had excellent instructors in preaching and outstanding colleagues in our preaching labs. We all longed to be faithful and effective preachers of God's word. Why couldn't there be a way to take all the theological and biblical expertise we had gained in our classes and bring it to bear in the pulpit? Was there no way to integrate our classroom learning into the craft of preaching? Certainly there was a way.

Never one to sit around and be content with what I considered a less than ideal situation, I sought out the fine teacher of rhetoric at the seminary, Gracia Grindal, to lead me to some resources for preaching that went beyond what was being offered in the classroom. Gracia introduced me to the work of Walter Ong, whose work on orality was my first glimpse into the difference between written word and spoken word, and with that, I was off and running.[1]

Continuing my studies in preaching during my first call, I began to discover an entire cadre of brilliant teachers who had been transforming the homiletical landscape for at least a decade. Indeed, they already had a name—they were called teachers of the New Homiletic. Fred Craddock, the diminutive, bespectacled Methodist from Georgia was leading the charge, with his method on inductive preaching.[2] Along with him was Eugene Lowry, a Disciples of Christ teacher, whose book *The Homiletical Plot* gave an actual pattern for sermon design that took into account the different reactions a listener might have throughout the sermon event. Then there was David Buttrick, the homiletician at Vanderbilt Divinity School, who gave us his famous *Moves and Structures*, and on and on it went.[3] During my first years in parish ministry I attended workshops with most of the pioneers of the New Homiletic and learned from their disciples, as well (Charles Campbell, Barbara Brown Taylor, Tom Long, James Forbes, and others). I learned that there was a brave, new world out there, paying attention for the first time, to the listener. What puzzled me was why my teachers at seminary hadn't introduced me to these new voices. Why was the New Homiletic not even discussed when

1. Ong, *Presence*.

2. Craddock, *Without Authority*. The 1st ed. of this classic work was published in 1974.

3. Other so-called pioneers of the New Homiletic were Henry Mitchell and Charles Rice, identified as such by O. Wesley Allen Jr., editor of *Renewed Homiletic*.

it was clearly a major movement among preachers in America? Wouldn't that have been helpful in bringing into the pulpit all the knowledge we had gained at seminary?

It wasn't until I began my Work in the doctor of ministry in preaching program at the Lutheran School of Theology at Chicago that I finally received the answer to my question. My thesis centered on the place of the listener in the sermon event.[4] In the course of my research I came across Karl Barth's writings on homiletics that were part of his debates with Emil Brunner in the 1930s. In these writings Barth made it very clear that preachers needed to remove themselves as much as possible from their preaching, so as to let God's word do its saving work. They were not to insert stories or anecdotes or other clever ways of making connections with people, lest the congregation be distracted from what God was up to.[5]

What I understood Barth to be saying was that rhetorical tools were of no help in reaching the listener. What people needed, according to Barth, was not artfulness, but an encounter with the living God. He viewed these two as mutually opposed to one another; i.e., you could not be artful as a preacher without getting in the way of the listener's encounter with God!

That is not to say that Barth was unconcerned with the listener, as his later works would show, yet the effect was that for generations, preachers were pretty much forbidden from working on their craft. They were expected to be excellent theologians, exegetes, and teachers, but rhetoricians? Never!

The results were predictable. Heinz Zahrnt, writing before the introduction of the New Homiletic, summarized things this way: "The effect of Barth's theology has been twofold. On the one hand, without it present-day preaching would not be so pure, so biblical, so concerned with central issues, but on the other hand, it would also not be so alarmingly correct, boringly precise, and remote from the world."[6]

4. See Monson, "A Funny Thing Happened."
5. Barth, *Homiletics*.
6. Zahrnt, *Question*, 118.

Upon reading Zahrnt's analysis of the Barthian effect on preaching, I finally had my answer as to why I hadn't been exposed to the New Homiletic at seminary: We Lutherans (at least in the upper Midwest) were still beholden to the Barthian view of preaching, even though the rest of the preaching world had left it behind. My fine teachers were still under the thumb of the tradition that said, in effect, "Faithful preachers do not concern themselves with artfulness!"

Ironically, I remember a member of the faculty telling me that one of the chief topics of conversation at faculty coffee time on Monday morning following chapel was to complain about the previous Sunday's sermons that they had heard. Whether they were complaining about them being boring or theologically suspect, or both, I'm not sure!

As years have gone by—and I have now been at this business of preaching for almost twenty-five years—I have preached and heard hundreds of sermons. Today virtually all of those sermons show the influence of the teachers of the New Homiletic. There is a constant concern for the listener: how to engage them, how to connect with them, how to "bring home" the message of the day. In fact, the emphasis today is so completely on the *craft* of preaching, that I have begun to wonder if the *theology* that should underlie our preaching has been lost. I have begun to suspect that Barth's fears are being played out as people encounter *artfulness*, but do not encounter *God*.

My goal in this book is to bring together both of these concerns: the concern that we must connect with the listener *and* the concern that we must be grounded theologically.

Particularly, I am concerned that we are firmly grounded in our treasured Lutheran imperative—rightly distinguishing law and gospel. I believe that by taking fully into account the treasures of Law and Gospel thinking and combining them with the insights of the New Homiletic school, we can be preachers who are not only artful, but also ones who while being true to the word, can facilitate an authentic encounter with the living God.

I have included footnotes throughout the book for you scholarly types who may want to read every jot and tittle on a particular topic. For those of you more inclined, as I am, to be found on the golf course on a warm spring day than in a reading chair, you can skip the scholarly stuff and proceed on so as not to miss your tee time! This guide is not meant to be exhaustive, but only supplemental to many other fine books on preaching that are undoubtedly already a part of any serious preacher's library. This book is meant to be a practical way to think about how one might go about proclaiming law and gospel in an engaging manner.

I have made a few assumptions. You have picked up this book because: (a) you want to become a better preacher; (b) you want some help with Law and Gospel preaching; (c) you are just beginning your preaching ministry and need a few ideas as to how to proceed; or (d) you collect preaching books. Any of these reasons are okay by me. Just remember, what we do as preachers, and what results from it are among God's mysteries. True preaching is always God's work not ours. As Barbara Brown Taylor has said, "There is more going on here than anyone can say. Preaching is finally more than art or science. It is alchemy, in which tin becomes gold and yard rocks become diamonds under the influence of the Holy Spirit."[7]

We can certainly improve our chances of being effective preachers by study and practice, but it will never be truly our work. In this book I have condensed a quarter century of my conclusions on this topic. I invite you to ponder them, wrestle with them, disagree with them, or nod in approval, with the hope that in so doing your own quest to be used by God in this mysterious work will be furthered. But even after reading this book I have no doubt that preaching will remain for you, as it is for me, a mystery. I'm okay with that. Blessings.

7. Taylor, *Life*, 85.

1

Law and Gospel Thinking

To BEGIN THEN, WHERE did this whole concept of Law and Gospel come from? From the Bible? Actually, no, at least not explicitly. Just as there is no place in the Bible where the term *Holy Trinity* is used, there is no place in the Bible where the term *Law and Gospel* is used. Though we will not find the Trinity named, per se, we will find lots of references to Father, Son, and Holy Spirit. So with Law and Gospel; though we will not find this phrase listed, we will find plenty of passages related to law and plenty of other passages related to gospel. Indeed, they are everywhere.

The Apostle Paul gives us perhaps the closest thing to an argument concerning law and gospel in the letter to the Galatians when he states, "For if the inheritance comes from the law, it no longer comes from the promise [the gospel]; but God granted it to Abraham through the promise" (Gal 3:18). It is evident that Paul's whole frustration with the Galatians is that, as Luther would say centuries later, they are not "rightly distinguishing law and gospel." In his closing statement Paul lays it all out: "You who want to be justified by the law have cut yourselves off from Christ; you have fallen from grace" (5:4). Later he warns, "Whoever it is that is confusing you will pay the penalty" (5:10).[1]

---

1. All references unless otherwise noted are from the New Revised Standard Version of the Bible (NRSV).

What Paul is talking about is the argument over the necessity of circumcision for Gentile believers, and while that is certainly no longer an issue for the church, today we see other confusions of law and gospel. Whenever it is announced that a person must have a particular experience or a particular testimony or what-have-you—in addition to Christ—in order to be saved, we have a confusion of law and gospel. The issue of rightly dividing law and gospel is already coming into play in the early church and continues to plague us up to the present day.

Augustine and Luther

Historically, St. Augustine would be the first theologian to actually tackle the subject in any thorough manner. Apparently he had some very studious folk in his congregation who paid close attention to the implications of his theology. To answer a question from a particularly scholarly parishioner, Augustine produced his treatise *On the Spirit and the Letter* in 412 where he gives his most extensive discussion of law and grace.[2] While Augustine's work does not quite get us to the full-fledged distinction between law and gospel that Luther offers, he does send us well on our way, showing the necessity of grace and the inability of the law to make us righteous. Augustine puts into play what Lutherans would later call the second use of the law, whereby the law reveals our willful disobedience and drives us to Christ.

It is left to Martin Luther, who begins regularly to insist on the need of believers—especially preachers and teachers—to rightly distinguish between law and gospel. In a sermon preached in 1525

2. Cary, "Lutheran Codicil," 5. I am indebted to Phillip Cary, who in an article entitled "The Lutheran Codicil" points out the difference between Augustine's law and grace, and Luther's law and gospel. He argues that while there are many common themes, Augustine omits a key Lutheran theme: "nothing less than what the mature Luther calls 'the gospel of Jesus Christ.'" Cary says that "Luther distinguishes law and gospel, Augustine distinguishes law and grace. The difference is encapsulated in what I call 'The Lutheran Codicil' to the Augustinian heritage, in which Augustine's insistence on fleeing for grace becomes Luther's insistence on fleeing to the gospel."

entitled "How the Christian Should Regard Moses" he gives a very clear statement on what the law is and what the gospel is:

> The law commands and requires us to do certain things. The law is thus directed solely to our behavior and consists in making requirements. For God speaks through the law, saying, "Do this, avoid that, this is what I expect of you." The gospel, however, does not preach what we are to do or to avoid. It sets up no requirements but reverses the approach of the law, does the very opposite, and says, "This is what God has done for you; he has let his Son be made flesh for you, has let him be put to death for your sake." So then, there are two kinds of doctrine and two kinds of works, those of God and those of men.[3]

It seems to me this is a basic distinction that is essential for us, as preachers, to understand. If we examine our preaching and find that primarily we are announcing to our listeners what *they* must do: have faith, love one another, follow Christ, chose the way of the Cross, and so on—all important and indeed biblical commands—then we must conclude that we are preaching primarily law, like it or not. For law is about what *we* must do.

On the other hand, if we examine our preaching and find that primarily we are announcing what *God* has done: Christ has died for you, God has forgiven you, God has claimed you in baptism, and so on—all essential words of grace—then we must conclude that we are preaching primarily *gospel*, like it or not. For gospel is about what *God* has done and is doing. The trouble with most of our preaching, however, is that it is often primarily one or the other. And our listeners need *both* the law and the gospel. The law without grace is cruel for it announces that finally our salvation is up to us. And the gospel without the law often becomes merely a recitation of God's loving attributes, with little power to elicit saving faith.[4]

---

3. Bachmann, "How the Christian Should Regard Moses," 162.

4. Braaten, *Principles of Lutheran Theology*, 112. Dr. Braaten's description is apt, that the gospel without law becomes "a saccharine-sweet message of civilizing aphorisms."

In America particularly, because of our seemingly inborn insistence on our ability to pull ourselves up by our own bootstraps, the former affliction, to preach primarily what is required of our listeners, is commonplace. Somehow we often end up preaching the message that the coming of God's kingdom among us is dependent upon our listeners just finally getting "serious" about the Christian faith. And so Sunday after Sunday we exhort people to pray more fervently, worship more regularly, believe more earnestly, sacrifice more deeply, and love more dearly. In effect, we say, "If you would just be more like Jesus, all of your problems and the problems of the world would be solved." Of course there is truth in this, but the problem is that there is no way any of us can be "more like Jesus" aside from Christ, himself, putting to death everything within us we call self and becoming our very life. And so these exhortations are fruitless and finally cruel because they call out to the one drowning in the boiling sea, "Swim harder!" when already the victim is drifting helplessly toward the bottom of the sea.[5]

Gerhard Forde

Gerhard Forde, longtime, beloved teacher at my alma mater, reminded us often of a further reason for the fruitlessness of preaching that appeals to human will or free choice. He insisted that the first presupposition a preacher must make is that our listeners are not only *unable* to do what the law requires, but they are *unwilling* to do it because their will is bound. Dr. Forde talked about our "god-project," our "upward rebellion," how, especially among us church folk, we are so easily seduced into believing that the life of

---

5. Kolb and Wengert, "Augsburg Confession," in *Book of Concord*, 57. Article 20 reminds us: "For without faith human nature cannot possibly do the works of the First or Second Commandments. Without faith it does not call upon God, expect anything from God, or bear the cross, but seeks and trusts in human help. Consequently, all kinds of urges and human designs rule in the heart when faith and trust in God are lacking. That is why Christ said (John 15 [v. 5]): 'Apart from me you can do nothing.' And the church sings: Without your will divine/Naught is in humankind/All innocence is gone."

faith is all about God helping us "be all we can be."[6] We treat God like our genie in a bottle who will grant us our every wish so that we can fulfill our destiny as children of God. Hidden from us, in this way of thinking, is that the stronger and stronger we grow, the less we need God, until finally when all is accomplished we are our own god! Now there is something truly demonic! So the irony of our striving after God in this god-project is that we finally end up, *by our own will*, estranged from God. We end up proving the truth of the inverse of the Apostle Paul's words: "When I am strong, then I am weak."

The gospel without law is also commonplace in America. It is not the call to vigorous Christian living that is the problematic tactic here, but an appeal to sweet statements of a supposed "gospel." As preachers in this mode, we often pepper our sermons with phrases like "God loves you" and "God forgives you" without the slightest mention of the costliness of that love or why that forgiveness is no less than a divine miracle. Our listeners are left, therefore, understanding that to *believe* this "gospel" is to somehow assent to these notions in a merely intellectual, passive sort of way, without ever being drawn into the radical, world-changing claims that the gospel has on us. It is here that we must recall the words of Jesus who acknowledged that even the demons believe and shudder, but that does not mean they experienced the all-encompassing power of the gospel.

Again, my teacher Gerhard Forde is very instructive in his remarks reminding us that believing the gospel is not simply an intellectual assent to a "formula." Believing the gospel is not, as the story goes, where the young boy came home from church and said, "Now I get it. I like to sin, and God likes to forgive sin, so we're both happy!" No, believing the gospel is a life-changing event akin to having the jury pronounce you innocent in the courtroom.[7]

6. Forde, *Theology Is for Proclamation*. For a thorough discussion of Forde's thought on law and gospel in preaching there is no better source than this text.

7. Forde, *Law Gospel Debate*, 74–75. As Forde says, "[The event of the cross] must be so conceived that faith for the believer is not merely belief in a theory *about* the cross, but a real *participation* in the event of deliverance itself . . . In other words, the paradigm for faith is not an act of cognition, the

Piortr Malysz, a brilliant young scholar teaching at Beeson Divinity School, speaks about another new sort of "gospel" that is currently being preached in America. He names it "the call to be oneself." He says that this gospel is supposed to be freeing because it does not announce the need for constraints other than those we impose upon ourselves in order to achieve self-realization.[8] The irony, of course, is that we are very competent and compulsive jailors. When the call comes to us to just "be ourselves" we find ourselves running off, endlessly pursuing what that means for us. It is, as Malysz says, "a never-ending pilgrimage of self-realization." In this case, this gospel is also cruel and fruitless, and becomes, in effect, another variation on the law.

Luther Continued

Returning to Luther, we see that he explores how the law and the gospel function in the lives of human beings. In his lectures on Galatians—certainly Luther's most extensive discussion of Law and Gospel—he speaks of how beneficial and necessary the law is. He says that without the law the self is left with the "presumption of righteousness"—a singularly dangerous place to be.[9] So Luther quotes the prophet Jeremiah saying the word of God becomes the hammer that breaks apart this huge rock. It breaks this rock of self-reliance by showing each person his or her failures before God. It

---

acceptance of a theory, but death and resurrection, participation in the event itself. The life of faith is a life of participation, a life in the 'body of Christ.'"

8. Malysz, "Third Use of the Law," a lecture given on August 15, 2012, at Calvary Lutheran Church, Golden Valley, Minnesota. This lecture is now available in print in a book entitled *Preaching and Teaching the Law and Gospel of God*, ed. Carl E. Braaten.

9. Pelikan, "Galatians," 310. "For as long as the presumption of righteousness remains in a man, there remain immense pride, self-trust, smugness, hate of God, contempt of grace and mercy, ignorance of the promises and of Christ. The proclamation of free grace and the forgiveness of sins does not enter his heart and understanding, because that huge rock and solid wall, namely, the presumption of righteousness by which the heart itself is surrounded, prevents this from happening."

functions like an MRI test, showing the deadly tumor lying in the tissue, enabling the patient to see what is really going on and driving her or him to the Great Physician for healing.

Later in this same lecture Luther goes even further, clarifying what this means for us, teaching us that God is not like some sadistic pagan god that delights in revealing our faults to us. No, rather God reveals our faults so that we may be released from them. God reveals our sickness so that we may be healed. God reveals our bondage so that we may be set free![10]

This is a very important point for us preachers to ponder. We must ask ourselves: What is our posture vis-à-vis our listeners when we preach the law? Do we delight in exposing their sins? Do we get a rush from understanding that some of our parishioners have a perverse delight in being scolded? Are we seduced into thinking that somehow God has privileged us with being able to stand apart from these poor sinners entrusted to our care and announcing to them *their* sins?

If we preachers have found ourselves ever praying the prayer of the Pharisee, "I thank you, God, that I am not like other folk," then Lord, help us. For the fact is, we are *exactly like* other folk, and that fact alone should make us humble, reluctant, and even sorrowful preachers of the law. Even as we preach the law faithfully, exposing the sins of our flock, we should grieve that we must do this, akin to parents who grieve when they must discipline their children severely for their own sake. We must remember that our call is not to bring shame upon our listeners, that is, to create self-loathing in them, but rather to cause them to loath sin in their own lives. Our goal is not for them to despair, but for them to see clearly that their sins are robbing them of life, joy, and freedom, and that Christ is the only way to recover life, joy and freedom.

---

10. Ibid., 339. "For God does not want to trouble you in such a way that you remain in trouble; he does not want to kill you in such a way that you remain in death. 'I have no pleasure,' he says through the prophet, 'in the death of the sinner' (Ezek 33:11). But he wants to trouble you so that you may be humbled and may acknowledge that you need the mercy of God and the blessing of Christ."

I have sometimes run into preachers who do not seem to understand the difference between shaming listeners and showing them their sin. It is understood most easily, I believe, by returning to the idea that the law is like an MRI test—it shows the deadly thing within. When patients see a tumor lying in their flesh, their instinct, it seems to me, is to want it removed, not to think, "My body is worthless." So it is with the law, properly preached. It drives listeners toward the Great Physician; it does not make them believe themselves worthless. It seems to me the law functions most effectively when the listener says to himself or herself, "That's *me* the preacher is speaking about today. That's *my* sin that is being preached about." When the congregational members are nodding in silent, sad recognition, then the law is doing its proper work, for it is not leading the people into despair, but leading them to understand their need for forgiveness and grace. But even this task we must enter into humbly, not wishing to hurt those who must endure this, but preaching this word of law out of genuine love for the folk who will hear it, and understanding that we, the preachers, are also afflicted with the same sins.

When we participate in this whole business of rightly distinguishing law from gospel, we begin to understand that this distinction is not important merely because it proves we are careful theologians. Neither is it important merely because we Lutherans are people of a Law and Gospel heritage that the church sorely needs in this day of alternative gospels. This right distinguishing of law and gospel is important because when the law is rightly preached people actually do understand their need for Christ. And when the gospel is rightly preached, people actually are freed from their sins. In other words, life-changing events happen to listeners who hear the law and the gospel preached! They are not sent once again into the frustrating and futile task of being their own savior. They are not told once again that if they would only get serious about the Christian faith—only believe more deeply and love more dearly—they would know the freedom of Christ. They are not simply given a series of impotent platitudes that do nothing to free them from sin or anxiety. No, they are actually led to repentance, forgiven and freed! They are, in a word, saved. Or in the words of John's gospel, they are "born again." What gift could be greater than this![11]

What we are doing then, as preachers, when we rightly distinguish law and gospel, is actually freeing the Word to do its work.[12] I like Dietrich Bonhoeffer's image where he says that when the gospel word is rightly preached Christ is present walking about among the congregation bearing its sins and burdens.[13] What a lovely image this is: Christ present among the people of God, hearing their confessions, embracing them in their sorrows, pronouncing to them the forgiveness of their sins, and sending them forth to live and serve in his name. If our preaching does that, then indeed it is worthy of its calling.

11. Ebeling, *Luther*, 117–18. "If the process of preaching is what it claims to be, that is the process of salvation, then as the distinction is made between the Law and the Gospel, so the event of salvation takes place. And a confusion of the two is not a misfortune of little significance, a regrettable weakness, but is evil in the strict sense, the total opposite of salvation . . . The failure to distinguish the Law and the Gospel always means the abandonment of the Gospel, leaving only the Law."

12. I want to be very clear here that when I use the term *Word* I mean much more than merely the Bible. I mean the Word in the Johannine sense, as in John 1 where we hear the writer say, "In the beginning was the Word, and the Word was with God, and the Word was God." This Word is the living, active, dynamic life through which God is at work in and through the spoken word of God. As the writer to the Hebrews reminds us: "Indeed, the word of God is living and active, sharper than any two-edged sword, piercing until it divides soul from spirit, joints from marrow; it is able to judge the thoughts and intentions of the heart" (Heb 4:12). I will repeatedly use this term to refer to the way God is at work in a text.

13. Bonhoeffer, *Worldly Preaching*, 29.

2

Law and Gospel Exegesis

BEING A LAW AND Gospel preacher begins at the very beginning of the sermon process, as we open our Bible and first look at the Scripture that has been appointed for the day. Notice, right away, we begin with Scripture. Law and Gospel sermons *always* begin with Scripture, and for those of us who are lectionary preachers— narrative lectionary or Revised Common Lectionary (RCL)—that usually means that we have a group of texts that have been appointed for that day.

As we begin work on the sermon, we must bear in mind the fundamental insight that the Law and Gospel paradigm offers us: The law and the gospel function differently in the lives of our listeners. That is to say, rightly preached, the law produces one thing and the gospel another in those who hear these words.

Luther defined the law as that which tells us what God expects of us and the gospel as that which we can expect of God. In this paradigm the law functions to *instruct* us, and the gospel functions to *free* us.

Another way the law and gospel function, especially according to what Lutherans have called the second use of the law, is that the law produces in us a recognition of *being lost* and the gospel produces a recognition of *being found*. Or in one of the simplest ways I have heard of summarizing this, the law says, "You need

Christ!" and the gospel says, "Here is Christ!" These are different functions. The law drives the believer towards Christ; the gospel frees the believer from guilt and sin.

Because these two functions are so integral to the whole enterprise, it is important for us, at the very beginning of the examination of the text, to look at how the Word is functioning in the particular pericopes that have been assigned for the day. And when I say "the Word" it could be the way the story functions, or the way the prophet speaks, or the way the psalmist writes, or the way God works, or the way Christ is at work, or even the way the Spirit is at work in the text. There are multiple ways that the *living Word* functions in a text.

What's the Word Doing?

As a starting point, let us look at the lessons for the beginning of the season of Pentecost in the year of Luke, beginning with the Festival of the Holy Trinity. The texts assigned for this day are Proverbs 8:1–4, 22–31; Romans 5:1–5; and John 16:12–15. In the first lesson, Wisdom is speaking in the first person, rejoicing that she was there at creation. In the second lesson, the Apostle Paul witnesses to the fact that "God's love has been poured into our hearts through the Holy Spirit that has been given to us." Finally, in the gospel lesson, the writer assures us that "when the Spirit of truth comes, he will guide [us] into all truth." So we could lay out how the Word functions in these three texts in the following way:

Prov 8:1–4, 22–31—Wisdom rejoicing

Rom 5:1–5—God's love given through the Holy Spirit celebrated

John 16:12–15—Promise of the Holy Spirit's guidance given

With this basic sketch in mind, we have a starting point and a goal, for we know now what the goal of our sermon on any one of these texts must be. If we choose to preach only on Proverbs, then the goal of that sermon must include a genuine sense of rejoicing that Wisdom was there at God's creation. Or if we choose to preach only on the second lesson, our goal will include a celebration of the gift of God's love given to us through the Holy Spirit. And similarly, if we preach only on the gospel from John, we will be sure to include the promise that the Holy Spirit will be given to our listeners who will guide them into all truth.

What Does "What the Word Is Doing" Have to Do with Us?

Before we get too far along, I need to clarify one thing: What does "what the Word is doing" have to do with us? Answer: Everything! What the Word is doing in the text is what we, the preachers, must do in the sermon!

This is one of the most important tenets of Law and Gospel preaching. Gerhard Forde called this "doing the text" to the hearers.[1] Forde was always very insistent that when a preacher preaches a sermon, that sermon must, must, must, *do* to the people what the text is doing to its hearers! As he famously said in class, "No one cares what *you* think about God; they care what *God* thinks about them!" Hence his insistence that we *do* the text to the people.

Now, of course, it can be seen immediately that such a beginning does not get us wholly to the place we must arrive—the place where the law and gospel do their work—nevertheless, to recognize how the Word is functioning in a particular text is supremely important.

More Examples of What the Word Is Doing

Let us look now at the texts for the Second Sunday after Pentecost in the year of Luke. They are 1 Kings 8:22–23, 41–43; Galatians 1:1–12, and Luke 7:1–10. In 1 Kings we hear the prayer of Solomon asking that the prayers of the foreigner be heard by God. In the lesson from Galatians, Paul is rebuking the people for deserting him

1. Forde, *Theology*, 155.

and turning to a different gospel that is contrary to the gospel of Christ. And in Luke we see Jesus announcing that the centurion's faith is beyond anything he has seen in Israel and granting the centurion's request that his servant be healed. So again we could lay out the functions of the Word in the following way:

1 Kgs 8:22–23, 41–43—Petition to God to hear the faithful prayers of foreigners

Gal 1:1–12—Strong rebuke of those who follow a different gospel

Luke 7:1–10—Praise of faith and an announcement of healing

Given this guidance, we see a sketch of what will be our task as preachers. If we choose to preach the Galatians text, our task will include a strong rebuke of those who stray into false gospels. If we choose to preach on the gospel text, we must include a lifting up of faith as praiseworthy in God's eyes, as well as an announcement of healing. And if we preach on 1 Kings we will be sure to include a prayer to God, asking that the prayers of all faithful people be heard.

One of the most common tendencies for preachers of all stripes is to understand what the Word is doing in the text, but somehow to end up preaching the law anyway. For instance, in the Luke text above, we have noted that Jesus praises the centurion's faith and heals the centurion's slave. This is how the divine Word functions in this text—Jesus being the Word. But instead of announcing to the congregation that Christ has come among them and healed them, despite their unworthiness—as he did for the centurion's slave in the text—we end up exhorting our listeners to have more faith.

Jesus did nothing of the sort in the text. He praised faith. And yet we often somehow conclude that our job is tell people to have faith, as though that is what creates faith. No, what produces faith is the announcement of the gospel: "You are healed. You are forgiven for Jesus' sake. You have been saved through faith." Saving faith is a gift that comes when the gospel is preached. As Paul reminds us, "So faith comes from what is heard, and what is heard comes through the word of Christ" (Rom 10:17). Saving faith does not come to our listeners by exhorting them to have faith. This tendency to take a text where the Word—in this case, Jesus—is very clearly announcing healing and turn it into an exhortation to faith is very common. This is an example of taking a gospel text (God's action of grace) and turning it into a law sermon (our action required). There are pitfalls in nearly every text, for it is rare that a text is fully law *and* gospel, self-contained.

The Third Sunday after Pentecost in the year of Luke, gives us 1 Kings 17:17–24, Galatians 1:11–24, and Luke 7:11–17, a continuation of the readings from the second week. In the first lesson we have the revival of the widow's son through the prayers of Elijah. In the second lesson we have Paul's narrative of how God revealed the gospel of Christ to him during his three-year sojourn in Arabia. Finally, in the gospel we have Jesus raising the dead son of the widow of Nain. The three functions of the Word are as follows:

1 Kgs 17:17–24—God answers prayer resulting in resurrection

Gal 1:11–24—Testimony of the divine origin of the gospel

Luke 7:11–17—Jesus has compassion on the widow and raises her son

This Sunday includes two miracle texts, both stories of resurrection. In the 1 Kings account we read that the boy has "no breath left in him" and in the Luke account that Jesus is actually meeting the funeral procession with the boy on the bier. When we encounter texts that announce resurrection, undoubtedly we are given pause. We might well say to ourselves, "Elijah might have raised the dead, and Jesus surely could, but not me." And so, as preachers we shy away from the obvious function of the text. We see that the prophet and Jesus are raising people from the dead, but concluding that *that* function is beyond us as preachers we look elsewhere for a theme. And when we do this we typically end up with some sort of law, some sort of exhortation to godly living. For example, using the 1 Kings account we might point to Elijah's fervent prayer and say, "Here is your example, people of God. Pray fervently and God will do great things." Or using the Luke text we might point out the compassion of Jesus and say to our congregation, "People of God, you are called to compassionate living. And when you do this, God will do great things." Of course, these are both fine messages, but nevertheless they are an appeal once again to the listener to do more of what they already know they must do: pray and have compassion. The result is that the age-old message of the law returns: do more of what God requires, and God's kingdom will come among you. But this appeal once again frees no one from sin and guilt for it is an appeal to law and not gospel.

What we must consider on this Third Sunday of Pentecost is that God actually does raise the dead through our preaching. This may sound radical, but theologically nothing could be truer. For what does the writer of Ephesians assure us in the letter but that we are all dead in sin apart from Christ:

> You were dead through your trespasses and sins in which you once lived, following the course of this world, following the ruler of the power of the air, the spirit that is now at work among those who are disobedient . . . But God, who is rich in mercy, out of the great love with which he loved us even when we were dead through our trespasses, made us alive together with Christ—by grace you have been saved—and raised us up with him and seated us with him in the heavenly places in Christ Jesus. (Eph 2:1–6)

This is the move that we must make in *doing* this text to the people. We must see that our position in the text is not the position of Jesus or Elijah, but our position is that of the dead ones. We are the ones lying lifeless on the bed and the bier. We are the ones that the prophet prays over. We are the ones that Jesus breathes life into. Because of our sin, we are the dead ones. And when we see ourselves as those persons in the text, then we see how much we need God's divine miracle.

So in *doing* this text to the congregation we have the task of announcing to them, first of all, their place in the text: "You are the dead ones." This is, of course, the function of the law, and we can do this in multiple ways, but the task will be for us to get the listener to identify himself or herself as the one in need of resurrection. And then, when that is accomplished, we have the joyful task of announcing that God has heard the prayers of God's people, and Christ has come to raise us from the dead through the forgiveness of our sins. This then will be true to the function of the Word in the text, and it will also serve to bring to life the people of God who are dead in their sins. As one Scottish preacher reportedly said, in a deep Scottish brogue, "The purrrpose of prrrreaching is to rrraise the dead!"

The Fourth Sunday after Pentecost in the year of Luke presents the preacher with fresh challenges. The appointed texts are 2 Samuel 11:26—12:10, 13–15; Galatians 2:15–21; and Luke 7:36—8:3. The Old Testament lesson is part of the larger story of David's adultery and his murder of Bathsheba's husband, Uriah. The text appointed for the day gives only the confrontation between the prophet Nathan and David, nevertheless it functions to condemn David's action and then to announce God's forgiveness following his confession. The continuation of the Galatians reading gives us one of the central texts of this letter of Paul's, announcing to us the utter futility of trying to justify ourselves by the works of the law. Finally, the Luke text, similar to the Samuel reading, is a story within a story whereby the guilty pronounce themselves guilty. In the Samuel reading it was David who declared "the man who deserves this must die." In the Luke reading, Simon, the Pharisee, concludes that the one who has been forgiven more will love more, thus condemning his own lack of love. The unnamed woman in the text, however, who is showing Jesus great love and respect, is granted forgiveness and peace. We might diagram the functions of the Word in these texts in the following way:

2 Sam 11:26—12:10, 13–15—Sins condemned, confessed, and forgiven

Gal 2:15–21—Exhortation to abandon justification through works

Luke 7:36—8:3—Lovelessness condemned, love commended, sins forgiven

The gospel text and the Old Testament reading are unique in that in both of them the Word actually functions *both* as law and as gospel. In the reading from Samuel, David is confronted via a story with his own heinous sins. Nathan tells the story of a rich man who steals from a poor man out of sheer selfishness, and David announces that this man deserves to die. Then, in a move that David clearly doesn't see coming, Nathan declares, "You are the man!" In Luther's terminology the law here is clearly a hammer. It breaks the rock of David's hidden sins in pieces.[2] Nathan then continues, announcing to David the terrible consequences of his sins: the sword will not depart from his own house, and the child conceived in Bathsheba will die. If we follow the story to the end we see that David fasts and prays to save the child, but to no avail. However, David's sins are forgiven by God. As Nathan says, "Now the Lord has put away your sin; you shall not die." Our task in this text is clearly to do what Nathan does: to move our listeners to abandon any pretense of righteousness and to confess sins, and then to announce to them that the Lord has put away their sins "as far as the east is from the west" (Ps 103:12).

The gospel text functions similarly. Jesus is in the house of a self-righteous Pharisee named Simon. When an unnamed woman enters and begins to weep at Jesus' feet, bathing his feet with her tears and wiping them with her hair, Simon thinks to himself, "If this man were a prophet, he would have known who and what kind of woman this is who is touching him—that she is a sinner." In this self-disclosure Simon shows his lack of respect for Jesus and his view of himself as far above this sinful woman. Jesus, knowing the thoughts of Simon, tells him a story about two persons who have debts forgiven and he asks him, "Now which of them will love him more?" Simon answers, "I suppose the one for whom he cancelled the greater debt." And Jesus replies, "You have judged rightly." Then Jesus goes on to explain to Simon that he is the one in the story who has fallen short—he is the one who loves little. Like

---

2. Pelikan, "Galatians," 310. In this portion of Luther's lecture he writes an extended piece on the way the Law acts as hammer, fire, wind, and earthquake to attack our presumption of righteousness.

David in the Samuel text, Simon has pronounced himself guilty. The woman, on the other hand, whose sins have led her to weep at Jesus' feet, receives the gospel word, "Your sins are forgiven." The Word, in this case Jesus, functions both as law and gospel, with one obvious difference: the Word functions as law for one person—the Pharisee, but as gospel for the other—the unnamed woman. The challenging task of the preacher will be to move the congregation to identify themselves both with Simon—needing to put away self-righteousness, and the woman—receiving the word of grace.

The Plot Thickens

As I have mentioned, the two texts analyzed above are unique in that the Word functions as both law and gospel in each one, albeit somewhat differently. This leads me to a very important point that is clear to any preacher: Both the law and the gospel are often *not* explicitly present in every text.

How does one deal with this as a preacher? One way is to decide that the sermon for the day will *not* include both law and gospel. Perhaps we decide that on Holy Trinity Sunday we will simply celebrate the Triune God as the Word in the text does. Or perhaps on the Second Sunday of Pentecost, when faith is praised and healing is announced, we decide that will be the message for the day. We are still "doing the Word" to our listeners, still proclaiming God's work, so knowing our congregations and what they need to hear at any particular time, we may simply choose to go with either instruction or promise on any given Sunday.

If, however, we decide, that sermons containing both law and gospel are the urgent and regular need of our listeners, then we must deal with the fact that the Word does not function fully as law and gospel in all texts. This can be tricky to handle, but in the exegetical process we can often see what is happening in the text by identifying the character who is most clearly *experiencing* the power of the Word. In the gospel texts we have looked at so far, for example, we can see that the centurion and the healed slave in Luke 7:1–10 experienced the power of the Word. In the following story from Luke 7:11–17 the dead son experiences the resurrection power of Christ. And in Luke 7:36—8:3, both the weeping woman and Simon, the Pharisee, experience the power of Christ's words.

In each of these characters we can easily see which side of the law/gospel equation is missing from the text. In the case of the centurion, he announces his own need for grace, saying, "I am not worthy to have you come under my roof." This is our entrée into helping our listeners say this themselves, and then experience the power of grace that comes despite our unworthiness. In the case of the dead son, the sheer fact that the boy is dead is our departing point as we announce that we all are dead in our sins. And so it goes. If we follow the character who experiences the power of the Word, it will become clear to us which is missing from the text—law or gospel—and subsequently as we begin to develop the sermon, we will understand what needs to be added to the text to make the sermon complete.

One final word on how we relate to the function of the Word: It is always important that we, as preachers, also identify with the characters in the story who experience the power of the Word. We must make it clear to our listeners that we too stand under the power of the Word, whether it be law or gospel, and the Word has its way with us as well as with them.

A temptation of all preachers is to correctly identify the ones who are experiencing the power of the Word in the story, but then identify ourselves with the Living Word! We identify ourselves inadvertently, as Jesus, or God, or the Holy Spirit. This seems ludicrous, but it is a very common pitfall. We must be diligent in our sermon preparation to remain closely identified with those whom have experienced the Word.

What about Nonnarrative Texts?

Before continuing, a word about the second lessons. In the season of Pentecost in the year of Luke we have considered the following appointed texts:

Gal 1:1–12—Strong rebuke of those who follow a different gospel

Gal 1:11–24—Testimony of the divine origin of the gospel

Gal 2:15–21—Exhortation to abandon justification through works

The way the Word functions in these texts can be summarized in the phrases above, and the speaker of this word is the Apostle Paul. The difficulty in preaching these texts, or any epistle text for that matter, is that there is rarely a narrative plot to follow that the preacher can use to engage the listener. Eugene Lowry, in his classic book *The Homiletical Plot* writes about how important it is that a sermon has a plot, or a movement from tension to release.[3] Because this is the case, when we take up the task of preaching epistle texts we must often supply our own narratives and our own plot lines to engage our listeners.

In the Galatians texts above there is a thin plot line to begin with. In the first text we have Paul's lament: "I am astonished that you are so quickly deserting the one who called you in the grace of Christ and are turning to a different gospel" (1:6). We could perhaps use this personal lament, calling to mind the strong attachment Paul, the pastor, had to the congregations of Galatia. We could perhaps remind our congregation of Paul's hardships, recorded in the book of Acts, and how much he experienced bringing the gospel to the Galatian cities.

Likewise in the second half of chapter 1, in the second of these texts, we have a slim narrative of Paul's sojourn in Arabia. This too might be built upon as a vehicle for connecting with the listener. But as we get further into this book of Galatians, the language becomes more and more the language of theological argument, and this is where the difficulty lies. In writing a sermon on an epistle text, how do we form a plot line out of a theological argument? As I say, we are forced, in these cases, to supply our own

---

3. Lowry, *Homiletical Plot*. Lowry's students at Saint Paul School of Theology in Kansas City, Missouri, actually came up with five different expressions for the stages of a plot through a sermon. They are "Oops, Ugh, Aha, Whee, and Yeah." You can almost hear in those expressions the movement from the law to the gospel: from Ugh to Whee.

narratives. In doing so, again it is essential that we not fall into the typical sermon of exhortation, whereby we take on the role of the apostle. Rather, we must identify, in these cases, with the Galatians and lead the congregation to identify with them as well.

One other tactic in using epistles in preaching is simply to mine some of the rich imagery of Paul's letters, but not use them as the central text for preaching. For example, in the text from the second chapter of Galatians we have the imagery of being crucified with Christ, and no longer being alive except through Christ (2:19–20). This rich imagery can play a key role in a sermon when the central text is either the Old Testament or the gospel for the day.

Challenges Abound

The Fifth Sunday after Pentecost in the year of Luke offers still more unique challenges. The appointed texts are Isaiah 65:1–9, Galatians 3:23–29, and Luke 8:26–39. The Isaiah text is undoubtedly a text of judgment, though the opening verses indicate how reluctant God is to pronounce such judgment: "I held out my hands all day long to a rebellious people [but now] I will not keep silent, but I will repay; I will indeed repay into their laps their iniquities and their ancestors' iniquities together, says the Lord." The Galatians text is a continuation of the epistle, but instead of judgment the Word functions here to announce God's mercy: "For in Christ Jesus you are all children of God through faith. As many of you as were baptized into Christ have clothed yourselves with Christ." Finally, in the gospel text we have the story of the Gerasene demoniac. Here Jesus enters the scene and is immediately met by a demon who implores Jesus to refrain from tormenting him. As it turns out the demon is only the spokesperson for a host of demons that Jesus allows to enter a herd of swine and be drowned in a lake. Interestingly the people of the region respond in a similar way to the demons. Instead of marveling at the healing that has come to the man whom Jesus has freed from the demon, they beg Jesus to leave their country because they, like the demons, are "seized with a great fear." In this text the healing function of the Word is in the background while the terror created by the presence of the Word in both the demons and the people of the city is in the foreground. We then might diagram the function of the Word in these texts in the following way:

Isa 65:1–9—God's reluctant word of judgment

Gal 3:23–29—A celebration of faith's power to free us from the law

Luke 8:26–39—Jesus' presence brings fear and freedom

The gospel appointed for this Sunday brings a unique challenge in that Jesus not only exorcises a demon from the Gerasene man, but he creates great fear in two communities: the "community" of demons named Legion living inside the man, and the city in which the demoniac lives. Both are described vividly by Luke as living in great fear of Jesus' power. The demoniac, on the other hand, is freed of his demon almost as an aside and is described, following his exorcism, as "sitting at the feet of Jesus, clothed and in his right mind." The challenge for us will be to choose which of these characters to identify with. If we choose to identify with the people of the city then the task will be to draw our listeners into an experience of the fear those people felt at the presence of the Word. That would be one way of letting the Word function the way it does in the text. On the other hand, we could identify with the demoniac and seek to help the congregation experience the freeing power of the Word that leads a person into the posture of the freed demoniac: clothed, in a right mind, and sitting at the feet of Jesus. If we decide to do this, the imagery in the Galatians text comes into play quite nicely as Paul reminds us that in baptism we have been "clothed" with Christ. Whichever tack we decide to take, the task is to be sure to *do* what the text *does* as part of the sermon. If we choose to identify with the people of the city then the task is to have the congregation feel the same fear at the presence of Jesus that the people of the city did. Of course, we do not leave them there, but move on to announce the gospel word; nevertheless, in faithfulness to the function of the

Word, this first move must be made. And similarly, if we choose to identify with the demoniac, the task is to have the congregation experience what the demoniac experienced: freedom from their demons. This gospel work will not be accomplished, however, without the use of the law that first *shows* them their demons, so in this case, the work of the law must be added.

What this example points out is that we must be cognizant of how the Word is functioning in the text so that we can determine whether it is the law or the gospel that must be added in the crafting of the sermon. In the first scenario, described above, the Word is functioning in the text as law, causing fear in those who encounter it. Because of this, we must add the gospel word to the sermon in order to have the complete package of law and gospel. In the second scenario, the Word is functioning in the text as gospel, causing freedom to come to those who encounter it. Because of this, we must add a word of law to the sermon in order to have the complete package. This is often the way it is, since it is rare that the Word functions as both law and gospel in the same text.

Stuempfle's Word of Caution

A word of caution, however, is apropos here. As Herman Stuempfle so clearly showed in his foundational work on Law and Gospel preaching, the theological categories we are speaking about here are not merely cogs in some mechanism that we can easily adjust with our homiletical wrenches and then be assured that a fine sermon will result. In Stuempfle's words, the developing sermon is "a living entity," something akin to a child growing within the womb of the mother. The discerning of law and gospel in a text, and the right adding of one element or another in the development of the sermon, are essential to the healthy development of the life in the "womb" of the preacher, but the sermon remains a living being, created by the Spirit of God, and its final form will often be a surprise both to us and to our listeners. This is as it should be.[4]

4. Stuempfle, *Preaching*, 76–77.

The Old Testament lesson appointed for this Fifth Sunday after Pentecost is another example of a text that is incomplete in itself, although there are hints of both law and gospel in it. Note in the Isaiah text the reluctance of God in judging the people of Israel: "I held out my hands all day long to a rebellious people." We hear in this text the ardent desire of God that the people repent and receive the forgiveness and mercy of God. This is certainly a gospel word that tells us that God longs to be gracious. But then comes the word of judgment: "I will indeed repay into their laps their iniquities and their ancestors' iniquities together, says the Lord." The text is filled with these words of judgment, so it functions pretty much as a word of law. Our task, then, will be to do this judging work, bringing the listeners face-to-face with the fact that finally God does judge sin. However, again we will not leave our listeners there, but will bring in the word of the gospel, which announces God's great desire to have mercy. Other Old Testament texts such as Ezekiel 33, where the prophet reminds us that God's desire is that no one be lost, can be used to lift up the gospel word, even if the Old Testament alone is used as the source for preaching on this Sunday.

The Call to Obedience

The texts appointed for the Sixth Sunday after Pentecost in the year of Luke are 1 Kings 19:15–16, 19–21, the call of Elisha; Galatians 5:1, 13–25, a call to freedom in the Spirit; and Luke 9:51–62, the call to discipleship. These texts bring into play another issue that we must be cognizant of as we begin the exegetical process—what Stuempfle terms "the call to obedience."[5] In the Old Testament text the aging prophet Elijah throws his mantle over his successor-elect, and Elisha responds, "Let me kiss my father and my mother, and

5. Ibid., 62–75. In this chapter Stuempfle does a very nice job of laying out the matter, saying that the preacher must "sound the call to obedience as a consequence of grace and not its cause." He points out that in Luther's well-known treatise, "The Freedom of the Christian" Luther calls us to "be Christs to one another." It seems to me that Stuempfle makes a good case for including the call to obedience in Law and Gospel preaching without getting into all the arguments about the third use of the law.

then I will follow you." Similarly in the Lukan text, a person called to follow Jesus replies, "I will follow you, Lord; but let me first say farewell to those at my home." To this Jesus says, "No one who puts a hand to the plough and looks back is fit for the kingdom of God." Clearly the function of the Word—whether it is Elijah's call or the call of Jesus—is the call to follow. It is not a word that explicitly reveals sin nor one that announces forgiveness. So once again, in faithfulness to the function of the Word in the pericope, we must issue the call to obedience at some point in the sermon. But then, what becomes of the words of law and gospel? In the case of these texts, *both* the law and the gospel must be brought into play, either from what is implied in the text or from outside the text. In the case of the law we might decide to lift up our bondage to "looking back" at all we fear we must give up if we follow Christ. What comes to mind is that tragic story of Lot's wife, as she looked back longingly at Sodom, even though Sodom was a place of evil and death. In announcing the gospel we might choose to announce that even though we, like those called by Jesus, are bound to our desires to have earthly comforts (e.g., a place to lay our head), to bury our dead, and to linger with those who would dissuade us from following Christ, yet God calls us. In any case, no matter what strategy we employ, it is essential for us to emphasize that we obey *because* of God's gracious call, not *in order* to obtain God's favor. In the chapter on sermon development to come we will explore this call to obedience further for it is an essential part of preaching and yet tricky, because it can so easily turn into an appeal to the law (i.e., "obey God and God's kingdom will come among you").

Once we have identified clearly the way the Word functions in the text and can see what must be added in order to achieve a complete Law and Gospel message, we have completed an essential task that will inform the eventual design of the sermon. Of course, there are other tasks important to exegetical work. It goes without saying that the exegetical process will necessarily involve many other partners and steps that will help enable us to clearly identify what is at stake in any particular text. Lively conversation with trusted colleagues in a text study, translation of the text from the original language, and exploring commentaries both hard copy and online, are all excellent and important methods for discerning the movement of the Spirit in any particular text.[6] The whole task of exegesis is to ask as many questions of the text, from as many perspectives as possible, in order to open up its meaning, so any method that achieves this is worthwhile. For example, I have found the questions posed in Mark Allan Powell's book *What Is Narrative Criticism?* very helpful for discerning the plot of a text.[7] Powell's work explores Scripture as you would a novel or a theater piece and asks questions about the event happening in the text, the characters involved, the setting, and the rhetorical devices used in the telling of the story. In the appendix to the book Powell summarizes his work and offers questions for using narrative criticism in exegesis. David Lose, in his book on preaching in the postmodern world also offers a series of questions that can open up a text for a preacher. They are questions that search for the claims that this text is making upon us or on our community.[8] Certainly every one of us will have our favorite go-to tools for doing exegetical work. The point, as Fred Craddock famously reminded his pupils, is to have a eureka, an "aha moment," where the text opens up before us and it begins to really speak to us. The second "aha moment" will come later as we discern how to best say what the text says, or in Law/Gospel parlance, to do what the text does.[9]

---

6. There are, of course, scores of commentaries on any book of the Bible. Several commentaries that I find helpful are the *Ancient Christian Commentary on Scripture*, ed. Oden, and the (still to be completed) *Reformation Commentary on Scripture*, ed. George. Also, online resources such as Workingpreacher.org, Textweek.org, and Christiancentury.org/RCL are often excellent sources of insight.

7. Powell, *Narrative Criticism*.

8. Lose, *Confessing*, 196–97. Lose asks questions such as: "What is this text trying to convince me/us of? What does this passage assert about the human condition and about God? How does this text seek to lay hold of me/us?"

9. Craddock, *Preaching*, 85. Craddock, a longtime professor of preaching at Candler School of Theology, Emory University in Atlanta was well known for reminding his students that they had two tasks in preparing to preach: to hear what the text was saying and to discover how to say what the text was saying. He called these the two eurekas, and he said that unless the preacher, in his or her preparation, had two eurekas it was unlikely the listeners would have even one!

3

Law and Gospel Design

WITH THE CENTRAL MESSAGE of the text or texts clearly in mind, as well as a clear notion of the way the Word is at work in these texts, we are ready to begin laying out the sermon. As any preacher knows, during the exegetical process there are bound to be many notions that come to mind that might serve as vehicles for the eventual shape of the sermon. We are wise to pay attention to these notions and make note of them, but being careful not to get too caught up in these notions early on, when the focus must be on the text itself. It is the woeful experience of every preacher to have been seduced by some alluring illustration or story, spend all our precious exegetical time attending to this beauty, only to discover at the end that it has nothing of substance to offer the final form of the sermon. So it is best simply to take note of any notions that come along, but let the text continue to be the focus of our exegetical work, and then in the end see if any of these ideas can be helpful in shaping the final form of the sermon.

Herman Stuempfle

One of the main contributions of Herman Stuempfle's work points out that when we begin to design a Law and Gospel sermon, we do not need to think only in terms of the law, or as Luther called it, "the hammer of judgment."[1] While it is certainly appropriate to conceive of the law as a hammer of judgment when approaching certain texts, there are other ways of preaching the law, and subsequently, other ways of preaching forgiveness, its gospel correlate. In exploring this subject, Stuempfle looked to the work of theologian Paul Tillich and homiletician Heinrich Ott who argued that contemporary listeners would be more likely to hear the law preached to them if, rather than a hammer of judgment, it was presented as a "mirror of existence."[2] They argued that the preacher could use such terms as "alienation, meaninglessness, brokenness, finitude, anxiety, and despair" rather than guilt to describe the contemporary situation, and so the law would function more like a mirror, showing the listeners their predicament, rather than a prosecutor, accusing them of wrongdoing. The function of the law would, in effect, then be "to expose" sin, rather than to judge sinners. Stuempfle called this the "horizontal dimension" of the law in contrast to "the vertical," and he called upon contemporary preachers to make frequent use of this dimension of the law by calling listeners to account for their lives and raising up for them the consciousness of their own lostness.[3]

Along with this call to preach the law differently than Luther would have preached it, Stuempfle argued that the contemporary preacher must preach the gospel differently as well, for with each manifestation of the law there is a proper correlate in the gospel. Hence, while forgiveness is the proper gospel correlate for the law preached as judgment, the proper correlate for the law preached as estrangement or anxiety is not.[4] Stuempfle suggested four different pairs of law/gospel correlates that we might use in the design of the sermon.[5] I have diagrammed them in the following way:

1. Stuempfle, *Preaching*, 21.
2. Ibid., 24.
3. Ibid., 25.
4. Ibid., 47.
5. Ibid., 49–58.

LAW AND GOSPEL DESIGN

Law	Gospel
Alienation	Reconciliation
Anxiety	Certitude
Despair	Hope
Transiency	Homecoming

So when designing the sermon, we simply decide which of these correlates to use, basing that decision primarily on how the Word is functioning in the text. For example if we were to take up a familiar text like the story of the prodigal son from Luke 15, we could readily see that the correlates of alienation and reconciliation might work well. So the design of the sermon could be to expose our willful alienation from the father in the preaching of the law, but then in the preaching of the gospel, show the father's reconciling love. This is quite a different tack than simply presenting the prodigal as a sinner in need of forgiveness, although this classic way of presenting this text might work well also. It is the combination of the text, our imagination, and the sense of our own congregation that will determine which correlates to use.

A text that might work well with the anxiety/certitude correlates is the gospel text appointed for the Seventh Sunday after Pentecost in Luke 10:1–11, 16–20. In this text Jesus is sending out the seventy, assuring them that they need "carry no purse, no bag, no sandals; and greet no one on the road." The function of the Word in this text is clearly to assure these disciples that God's provision will be sufficient for them, so likewise, we have this task in the sermon. The law in this case would function to expose the listener's anxiety over the stuff of everyday life—our preoccupation with full purses and fuller closets and even fuller bank accounts—and the gospel would function to assure the listener not to be afraid, for Christ is the Lord of the harvest and he has all things in his hands, and remind our listeners as well, that if "God so clothes the grass of the field, which is alive today and tomorrow is thrown into the oven, how much more will he clothe you—you of little faith!" (Luke 12:28).

Or looking at another classic text, the story of the good Samaritan from Luke 10, which is the gospel appointed for the Eighth Sunday after Pentecost in the year of Luke, we see that the Word is functioning in several ways. Jesus is functioning as teacher for the expert in the law who is attempting to justify himself, and the Word is functioning as healer in the person of the good Samaritan in the story. If we decide to take the position of the man in the parable who fell among the robbers, then we could well choose the correlates of transiency/homecoming for the design of the sermon, pointing out that Christ has bound up our wounds, poured out on us the wine of his own blood, and given us a place in the Father's house until he comes again on the last day. In this case the preaching of the law would function to expose our own woundedness and mortality, and the gospel would announce God's healing and provision for our salvation. Or if we decide to return to a classic tack and identify with the expert in the law who is trying to "justify himself," then the preaching of the law would function as a hammer of judgment that breaks down our attempts at self-justification, and the gospel would announce God's mercy even on us who attempt to take salvation into our own hands, for we "know not what we do."

A final example in this list of correlates might be the gospel text found in Luke 13:10–17 appointed for the Fourteenth Sunday after Pentecost in the year of Luke, where we hear the story of the healing of the woman who was bent over for eighteen years. Looking again at Stuempfle's choices we might well decide that the despair/hope correlates work well for this text. So in the design of the sermon, we would use the law to expose our despair at our own brokenness, but then show the work of Christ who loosens our bonds of despair, heals our brokenness, and gives us hope. Once again, in designing the sermon in this way, we are not avoiding the issue of sin and forgiveness, but simply presenting them in a different way that is both faithful to the text and the function of the Word in the text *and* hopefully effective in reaching the contemporary listener.

In all of these examples one can readily see that the pivotal turning point in each sermon design is the work of Christ. If alienation is the issue, then Christ's reconciling work is raised up. If anxiety is the malady, then God's provision in Christ is highlighted. If our transiency and mortality is exposed in the preaching of the law, then Christ's work of providing a place in the Father's house forever is the gospel correlate. If our problem is despair, Christ's ministry of mercy is lifted up. And, in a traditional rendering of a text, if the law functions to expose the sins of the listener, then God's work of forgiveness through the death of Christ must be preached. In each case it is *the work of Christ*, not the resolve of the sinner to try harder, which is preached as the antidote. This is vital to our preaching design, since our hope is not in our own strength or good intentions, but in Christ. Therefore, each sermon must be designed in such a way that Christ's work as savior, reconciler, mediator, healer, or whatever identity we choose, is lifted up as the solution to our lostness. There is no substitute for Christ's work!

Richard Lischer

Stuempfle, not surprisingly, is not the only homiletician to suggest a new set of correlates for the law/gospel sermon. Richard Lischer, another Lutheran teacher, has also suggested several pairs of possible law/gospel correlates for the preacher.[6]

Law	Gospel
Guilt	Justification
Debt	Forgiveness
Embattled	Victorious
Old creation	New creation

In his work Lischer points out that there are many biblical correlatives that one might select, but these are the four that he chooses to explore.

6. Lischer, *Theology*, 58–61.

Guilt and justification, Lischer's first pair, is the classic couplet that first the Apostle Paul and then Luther preached. In the Letter to the Romans, Paul lays out our problem:

> So I find it to be a law that when I want to do what is good, evil lies close at hand. For I delight in the law of God, in my inmost self, but I see in my members another law at war with the law of my mind, making me captive to the law of sin which dwells in my members. Wretched man that I am! Who will rescue me from this body of death? (Rom 7:21–24)

As Lischer points out, while contemporary psychologists have sometimes argued that guilt is a medieval malady, unknown to contemporary persons, our experience belies that pronouncement.[7] As preachers then, we still believe that it is appropriate that, with selected texts, this classic couplet continue to be employed in our sermon design. The gospel text appointed for the Eleventh Sunday after Pentecost in the year of Luke gives us a good example. In this text from Luke 12:13–21 we overhear Jesus telling the parable of the rich fool to a man in the crowd who wants Jesus to settle a family squabble over an inheritance. In response Jesus pointedly says, "Take care! Be on your guard against all kinds of greed; for one's life does not consist in the abundance of possessions." Since the Word here is functioning to point out our tendency to gather all things to ourselves, we might well decide that this text is a good place to put in play the guilt/justification couplet. In the sermon design, then, we would be sure to employ the law to do its work of causing our listener to conclude that "I am the rich fool. I am in bondage to gathering all things to myself." This would certainly be a way of causing guilt to arise in the listener's mind. Having done this, then we would be eager to announce the good news that Christ has come to rescue us from this body of death and to provide an abundant life that is far more glorious than anything we could ask for or imagine. We would then announce Christ's sacrifice for our justification and God's forgiveness for the sake of

7. Ibid., 59.

Christ. As always we would be careful to lift up the work of Christ as the antidote for the condition of greed, which has been identified, and not simply exhort our hearers to try harder to live their lives in generosity to others.

The debt/forgiveness couplet is similar to the preceding pair, although the term *debt* may imply that there has been an offense in the past that continues to linger and needs to be resolved. Debts are often piled up over time and when left unattended create havoc in our lives. A sermon design that uses this couplet would then attend to this scenario. A possible text might be Luke 16:1–13, the gospel text appointed for the Eighteenth Sunday after Pentecost in the year of Luke. In this text we meet the dishonest manager who, in the parable, seems to be in debt to everyone. Since his master has notified him that an accounting must be made, the dishonest manager goes to all his debtors and quickly cuts deals with them all, forgiving them much of their debt. We might, in designing a sermon around this tricky text, employ a strategy whereby the law is used to show our indebtedness in all things to God. God, after all, is the giver of everything we have, including our very life! For example, we might point out how God has forgiven us in Christ, even though we, like the dishonest manager, are completely unworthy of God's grace, or how God has blessed us with abundance beyond our deserving and yet we so often squander the Lord's goods. We could go on in multiple ways considering the many ways we are indebted to God. And then the gospel correlate could be to show that Christ has taken our place as debtor on the cross; that the Righteous One has taken the place of the unrighteous, and Christ has, as it were, scurried about, like the dishonest manager, paying all our debts.

Or another strategy for the same text might focus on the whole subject of faithfulness in small things, and so if we wanted to focus on this aspect of the text, then the first of Lischer's couplets—guilt and forgiveness—might be the best way to design the sermon. As always, we must study the text, listen to what the text is saying and how the Word is functioning within it, and *then* decide on the focus and the design of the sermon based on these things.

The rule is that our context, our study of the text, and our imagination are all used to inform the final decision.

Lischer suggests that the embattled/victorious couplet be used whenever we want to highlight the work of Christ in disarming the powers and principalities that hold us in bondage.[8] Texts that might be used in employing this strategy are the texts for the Sundays at the end of the Pentecost season, which are sometimes called the Sundays of End Time. In Luke 23:33–43, the gospel text appointed for the Last Sunday of End Time, Christ the King, we have an excellent opportunity to use this strategy. The crucifixion is beginning, along with the scoffing of the leaders and the mocking by the soldiers. Clearly the Lord is embattled at this point. But as the story unfolds and Jesus enters into conversation with the criminals hanging alongside him, we hear the words to the penitent thief, "Truly I tell you, today you will be with me in Paradise." The embattled Word, Jesus, is clearly victorious in the end. We could well design a sermon from this text showing how we are like the mockers or scoffers whom Jesus forgives, or how we are like the guilty criminals on the cross, who are either penitent or not. Or another strategy would be to take on the identity of the criminal who, though guilty and scoffed at by his fellow criminal, is embraced by Christ. In this way, the battles of the listener are lifted up, and the work of Christ that achieves the victory over all the powers and principalities, is made evident.

The texts appointed for the Sundays of End Time might also be an occasion for the last of Lischer's couplets—old creation / new creation. In Luke 21:5–19, the gospel appointed for the Third Sunday of End Time, Jesus is foretelling the destruction of Jerusalem. As he preaches outside the temple in Jerusalem and some of his listeners remark on the great beauty and majesty of the temple, Jesus says, "As for these things that you see, the days will come when not one stone will be left upon another; all will be thrown down." A sermon designed around this text could well highlight the old creation that is passing away. The Tillichian mirror could be employed to show how all things around us are passing away.

8. Ibid., 60.

All the people that surround us will pass away. All the stuff we have accumulated is wearing out and in decay. Even our own bodies are daily giving us evidence of the continuous march we are on toward the grave. We could point out that, unlike God, we are mortal, and all we have will someday be dust. But then the gospel correlate would be to announce Christ's promise that "not a hair of your head will perish." Hearkening back to John, we might remind our listeners that Jesus is the resurrection and the life and whoever believes in him though they die will live. The old creation does not have the last word, for as Paul says, "If anyone is in Christ, there is a new creation: everything old has passed away; see, everything has become new!" (2 Cor 5:17).

The Crossings Method

Another method I have found helpful in approaching the design of the Law and Gospel sermon is the Crossings Method.[9] This method was developed by Robert Bertram and Edward Schroeder, two former teachers at Concordia Seminary, St. Louis, who developed over many years an approach to designing a sermon that leads a preacher through various "stages" of law and gospel.[10]

One of the unique aspects of the Crossings Method is the three-level "diagnosis" of the human predicament in the law portion of the design and the three-level "prognosis," which is God's

9. The Crossings Community, Inc., according to its website (www.crossings.org), "is the corporate name of an international ecumenical group begun in St. Louis, Missouri, USA in the 1970s to engage in theological study and to relate that study to Christians' secular callings. The Crossings Method is a specific process for examining Scripture. Once we have listened to the Word of God, we set our lives next to it and connect them, 'cross' them, to understand how faith and daily life are interwoven. We study the Bible by: a) Looking for the text's own diagnosis of our human problem, then b) Checking the text once more for 'Good News' sufficient to solve that problem, and then c) Examining how the text actually brings the Good News to "cross" the problem and solve it."

10. By going to the Crossings Community website any preacher can view scores of sermon designs based on this method since a weekly text study using this method has been in place for many years and the results are archived from 1996.

response to this predicament, in the gospel portion.[11] According to this method (see diagram on page 39), in any text there is evidence or implication of trouble in the human condition. It might be greed, or lust, or pride, or unbelief, or any sin, hidden or unhidden, which is common to the human condition.

The first level of the diagnosis (D1) identifies what is called the "external problem," which is the obvious ways that this sin or malady makes itself known. At this level of analysis we ask the question: "What are the problem behaviors (i.e., thoughts, words, or deeds) that we can easily see when we come upon this condition?" In other words, what are the outward symptoms of this problem?

At the second level of the diagnosis (D2), we identify what is called the "internal problem." At this level of analysis we are no longer concerned with the outward symptoms—bad fruits—but with what is going on inside the heart of the sinner—bad hearts. The diagnosis at this level is done vis-à-vis the First Commandment, and this question is asked: "What do we fear, love, and trust?" Or another way of understanding this level is to ask the question: "What does this sin or sickness cause me to put my faith in instead of God?"

The third level of diagnosis (D3) is called the "eternal problem" and this has to do with the fact that finally all sin eventually separates us from God. Left unattended, sin always destroys us, or as Paul says, "the wages of sin is death" (Rom 6:23). It is the contention of the members of the Crossings Community that this is the level of diagnosis most often left out in contemporary preaching. We might well lift up the maladies of society and/or individuals and even suggest that they are more than a surface problem, but rarely do we venture to say that these sins create a separation between us and God. Rarely do we speak of our willful entrance into this separation, and even rarer is it for us to speak of God's condemnation or the sinner's lost condition before God.

---

11. This summary of the Crossings Method is from a lecture by the Rev. Marcus Felde at the Crossings Annual Conference on January 23, 2012.

But, of course, unless there is a condition from which a sinner needs to be rescued there is no need for a rescuer. And unless there is a condition from which a person needs saving there is no need for a savior. Finally, unless sin is really a very serious matter, there is no need for a sacrifice, thus there is no need for the cross. So the sad irony of this contemporary aversion to expose the eternal problem is that we often leave ourselves with no clear reason why we should preach the good news that Christ has come to rescue, to save, and to bestow forgiveness and righteousness on the unrighteous. The absence of an eternal problem actually eliminates the need for an eternal solution!

It is at this very juncture that the Crossings Method reveals its strength. For after exposing the eternal problem we move to the prognosis portion of the sermon design (P4) that is the "eternal solution." At this point we announce that God has done that which we cannot do: God has sent Christ into the world to save us from our lost condition, and we have been reconciled with God. As Ed Schroeder is fond of saying, "the sweet swap" has taken place.[12] On the cross, Jesus takes our sin, death, and misery and exchanges it for his righteousness, his life, and his joy. God "credits" Jesus' goodness to us. This is such a strong part of this design precisely because Christ is always central in providing the solution to the human predicament. If the problem is guilt, Christ pronounces forgiveness. If the problem is estrangement, Christ welcomes and embraces. If the problem is the old creation, Christ makes all things new. No matter what the sin, what the malady, what the predicament, Christ is the solution that moves us from the ranks of the lost and broken to the ranks of the found and made whole.

Another strength of this method is that the sermon design does not stop at the announcement of the good news, but doubles back on itself in the final two steps of the method. In the fifth step (P5) we are asked to revisit the issue of the heart from the

12. Dr. Edward Schroeder, one of the founders of the Crossings Community, tells that his teacher and later colleague, Robert Bertram, coined this phrase as an idiomatic rendering of Luther's "frolicher Wechsel," literally "jumping-for-joy exchange." Their work is very much grounded in the theology of Werner Elert.

diagnosis (D2) portion of the analysis, except this time rather than an internal problem we have an "internal solution," and instead of bad hearts we have good hearts. What we lift up at this point is the unique way in which the work of Christ has now made it possible for us to turn from false gods to faith in the one true God. By the power of the Holy Spirit (who is at work whenever we hear the gospel) we transfer our faith and trust from false gods to the true God. Because of the work of Christ, our hearts are changed—repentance! We are free to follow in a new way, which is the way of Christ.

And the final step (P6) identifies the ways in which we might now live out this new faith. Returning to the place where we began—the outward signs that showed our formerly lost condition—we now lift up the outward signs, the good fruits, which show the work of Christ within us. What was once an external problem now has an "external solution" that manifests itself in many ways as we become, as Luther said, "little Christs" to the world, sharing his saving good news by lives of witness and service.

So, for example, if in D1 (first stage diagnosis) the external problem was greed, in P6 (sixth stage prognosis) the external solution is generosity. Or if in D1 the outward manifestation of our sin is a lack of authentic hospitality to strangers, in P6 the new outward sign of Christ's work among is a radical welcome to all. In this way the method makes clear not only that Christ's work is central, but that Christ's work brings an observable change to our behavior and our life together as a community.

What can be seen, particularly in the final two stages of the Crossings Method, is that this method gets at the issue of Steumpfle's "call to obedience."[13] Sometimes referred to as the third use of the law, this call to obedience has often been a source of consternation for preachers, particularly Lutheran ones, as we have struggled mightily to avoid any suggestion that our works contribute to our salvation, and yet wanting to be clear that we are not advocating continuing in sin "that grace may abound." What the Crossings Method does so well is that it gives us a strategy

13. Stuempfle, *Preaching*, 62–75.

for preaching the call to obedience as a response to God's work in Christ. There is no suggestion that our works complete Christ's work or that apart from our response our faith is incomplete, but only that Christ's great work among us cannot but help bear good fruit in our lives. There is no sense then that we are advocating any new law for our listeners, but simply showing the way in which all things are new in Christ.

Following is a diagram that shows the movement from the external problem to the external solution. The design of the sermon is from D1 down the left side, crossing over from the eternal problem to the eternal solution, and then up the right side ending at P6. Notice that there is no way to cross from one side to the other apart from Christ.

Crossings 6-step Law/Gospel Method (for reading the Word and the world)	
Diagnosis	Prognosis
God sees through us using the X-ray of the *law*	God sees us through using the *promise/gospel*
D1: The External Problem *Bad fruits*	P6: The External Solution *Good fruits*
D2: The Internal Problem *Bad hearts*	P5: The Internal Solution *Good hearts*
D3: The Eternal Problem *Enemies of God*	P4: The Eternal Solution *Reconciled to God*
Christ's work makes this possible	

For example, the gospel text appointed for Christ the King Sunday in the year of Mark is John 18:33–37. In this text we hear Jesus announce to Pilate that "everyone who belongs to the truth listens to my voice." Using the Crossings Method, we might begin a sermon by noting the many ways that we belong. We belong to families, to clubs, to churches, to societies, and to cultures. We might suggest the many ways that this bears fruit in our lives, and furthermore the many ways that we must behave and we must conform to the groups to which we belong, lest we risk not belonging any longer. This would be the D1 portion of the sermon, revealing the bad fruits.

Moving onto D2, we might note that because we belong to a culture or a society or certain clubs or groups of people, we are in a sense controlled by them. They have certain expectations of what we may or may not do, and some of these expectations are opposed to God's expectations of us. Indeed, some of these expectations are downright destructive to ourselves and others around us. For example, there might be certain prejudices that are accepted or even encouraged. Or perhaps there are excesses in drinking or eating or forms of recreation (e.g., gambling) that are the norm in certain groups of people. Or perhaps some groups actually oppose the coming of God's kingdom among us by inhibiting acts of justice or environmental stewardship or the like. At this D2 level we are revealing our bad hearts.

From here we would move to the eternal problem (D3), that because we belong to the world, we are estranged from God. As Jesus said, "No one can serve two masters; for a slave will either hate the one and love the other, or be devoted to the one and despise the other" (Matt 6:24). Because God is not interested in sharing us with the world, by belonging to the world, we find ourselves outside of God's kingdom, looking in. This is our eternal problem.

At this point, the work of Christ comes to bear. We move to P4 and announce that because God is not interested in sharing us with the world, God sent Jesus Christ into the world to claim us as God's own. As Paul says, "God proves his love for us in that while we still were sinners [while we yet belonged to the world] Christ died for us" (Rom 5:8). In our baptism Christ says to us, "Child of God, you belong to me. You are mine. I will never let you go. You belong to me." We could spend considerable time here, showing the many ways that God has claimed God's people down through the ages, and now us through our baptism into Christ. This is God's eternal solution to our eternal problem.

From here, we move to P5 where we announce that because we now belong to God, through Christ's great work on the cross we are free to sever our ties with those who would try to lead us

LAW AND GOSPEL DESIGN

away from Christ. We no longer have to live up to the expectations of the world or the culture or the society in which we live, but we are free to live as servants of God. Our lives are now free to live in response to God's love, not in fear of what might happen if we don't measure up in the eyes of those who would control us apart from Christ. In this way, we speak of the way God creates new hearts in us, through a new sense of belonging.

Finally, in the final step of prognosis (P6), we might give a few examples of ways that our lives might reflect our new belonging. Perhaps as those who have been claimed by God we might be more inclined to refrain from excluding others or living our lives in prejudice and judgment. Or perhaps as persons who now are secure in our own belonging, we can reach out to serve and love those who also might have no sense that they belong to anyone or to God. In many and various ways we might suggest the good fruits that could be borne by such a new identity.

A Crossings Method diagram of this sermon could then be conceived of in this way:

John 18:33–37	
Diagnosis	Prognosis
D1: We belong to the world and must "behave"	P6: We belong to Christ and serve others
D2: Belonging means being controlled by the world	P5: Belonging to Christ, Christ controls us
D3: Belonging to the world, estranged from God	P4: God claims us as God's own in baptism
Christ's work on the cross takes us across	

Another text from John that lends itself quite well to the Crossings Method is John 2:1–11, the gospel appointed for the Second Sunday after Epiphany in the year of Luke, the story of the wedding at Cana. The pregnant phrase in this text is the statement by Jesus near the beginning of the story: "They have no wine."

Knowing that wine is the symbol for joy in the Old Testament, we realize immediately that this story, in typical Johannine fashion, is much more than a story about a miracle at a wedding; it is a parable about the abundance of God.

Employing the Crossings Method we might begin by noting the abundance of "empty water jars" we all have in our lives. As affluent North Americans, our lives our littered with stuff that is useless. We have attics and garages and homes bursting with junk that we neither need nor enjoy yet we hang onto it. Why? Lord only knows.

This abundance of empty things leads us to a deep longing for something that will fill us. And so we buy more stuff and search for finer things. Our hearts are seduced into believing that even though the stuff we have does not satisfy us, the next purchase will. Our faith is not in God, but in the stuff we have.

God's judgment falls on us as we finally realize that we have been duped by the world. The world around us has promised us joy and life and love and freedom, but it has not been able to make good on such promises. We find ourselves now truly without joy— we have no wine. And the God who makes the wine we need is only a distant memory, and we have none to turn to in our emptiness.

But God has not forgotten us. God sends the Son to the cross, and from that cross we hear the words that we thought only came from our mouths: "I thirst." Our Lord takes on himself the thirst we feel. Jesus experiences the emptiness and loneliness and desperation we feel when he also calls out, "My God, my God, why have you forsaken me?" And Jesus, with his own blood, fills the empty jars of our lives, forgives us our sins, and leads us out of emptiness into abundance.

Because Christ has broken the bonds of our addiction to empty stuff and given us the life that is truly life, we no longer seek to be filled by having more and finer things. Our faith is now no longer in the things that pass away, but in Christ. Because of this we experience abundance every day, no matter how much or little of the world's goods we actually own.

Our lives then, reflect this abundance of Christ. Instead of grasping incessantly for more and more of everything, we are content, and our lives are a constant giving not grabbing. Instead of living in fear that there may not be enough for us, we trust God's provision and share all we have. Instead of looking to the goods of the world to satisfy us, we enjoy them for what they are, but do not expect them to either give us life or joy or freedom or any of the gifts of God. God alone is our source of joy, and we no longer need ever say, "We have no wine."

Again we could diagram this sermon design using the Crossings Method in the following way:

John 2:1–11	
Diagnosis	Prognosis
D1: We live in scarcity amid abundance	P6: We live generously amid God's abundance
D2: We believe that our stuff will fill us	P5: We believe Christ leads us to abundance
D3: We thirst for God in our emptiness	P4: Christ takes our thirst upon himself on the cross
Christ's work on the cross fills us and takes us across	

The previous two examples of sermon design using the Crossings Method are certainly not the only ways that these two texts from John can be approached, but they do give a sense of how this method can be employed in bringing out a certain theme in a text. Again, the strength of this method is threefold: (1) it identifies the ways in which we have a problem with God—an eternal problem requiring an eternal solution; (2) it makes the cross of Christ central to the solving of our problem with God; and (3) it gets at the issue of obedience—the good fruits that we are called to bear—without causing any confusion regarding their bearing on our eternal relationship with God.

In the designing of the sermon, our task is to follow up the exegetical process with a clear notion of the strategy we will employ in getting at the heart of the text.

We must have in mind a clear idea of how the Word is functioning in the text and what we must add in order to complete the message of the sermon. Once we have this in mind, then the question is: "What is the clearest way to present the law and gospel—is there a couplet that can be used to bring out the unique way in which this text presents law and gospel?" Also, we must be sure to design the sermon so that Christ's work is the fulcrum on which the whole enterprise is hinged. Finally, the question of obedience must be addressed: What is the result in the listener's life of this saving work of Christ? Are there concrete ways in which the believer can "live out" the freedom that is made possible through this unique saving work of Christ? With all of these questions well in mind, and some notion as to how one will proceed, we are ready to write the manuscript.

4

Law and Gospel Manuscript Writing

THE MOST IMPORTANT THING to keep in mind when beginning to write a sermon manuscript is that the manuscript is not being written to be read. This might sound strange to say, but it is exactly the truth. A sermon is a *singularly oral event* and from the outset we must approach it as such. This means that what we write and how we write must continually take account of the oral nature of the sermon.

For me, this has always meant that I will not write something down that I cannot easily, at a later date, commit to memory, with the exception of short pieces of literature, poetry, or hymnody that I will actually quote in the delivery of the sermon. A good way to check oneself in writing the manuscript is to ask, "Is this something I can readily remember, or do I have to read this to deliver it?" If the answer is, "No, I can't remember any of this," we need to start again and rethink our approach, making sure we are cognizant that this is not a theological lecture, but a sermon. On the other hand, if the answer is "Yes, I can easily remember the flow, the major pieces of the sermon, the transitions, and eventual goal of the sermon," then we are on the right track.[1]

1. A major influence in my thinking on orality is the work of Walter J. Ong, SJ. His work *The Presence of the Word* gives a thorough description of the difference between a print culture and an oral culture. For example, the simple

Before we begin any sermon manuscript it is helpful to write three things at the top of the page: the *text*, the main *theme*, and the main *task* of the sermon, being sure that this task aligns with what the Word is doing in the text. Finally, we need to remember that the goal is for *our listeners* to be able to remember the sermon. If we cannot remember what we have written, it is most unlikely that the listener will be able to either. As Fred Craddock famously said, "The goal is not to get something *said*, but to get something *heard*."[2]

It seems to me that the writing of the manuscript is the place where the genius of the New Homiletic thinking really comes through.[3] The works of the pioneers of this movement all had one thing in common: They understood the sermon as an event in time.[4] The sermon was not, as it had been conceived of for centuries, a monologue delivered by a skilled rhetorician to a passive listener, but rather it was an event in which both preacher and listener were engaged in a divinely inspired discovery of what God was saying to them through the Word. In the New Homiletic the listener was conceived of as a partner, a co-participant or a fellow

---

fact that in an oral culture no one can look up anything has a profound impact on the society. Everything must be taught and learned orally and whatever is not remembered will not survive. Also, Ong points out the communal nature of an oral culture. A print culture creates the isolated thinker with a book, but the oral culture knows no such person, since all wisdom and knowledge is dependent upon relationships. Both of these aspects of oral culture have a bearing on my thinking of preaching as an oral event. Ong's later book, *Orality and Literacy*, builds on the insights of his earlier work. In this book he talks about how writing restructures our consciousness. Interestingly, he talks about how oral cultures do not trust print. They view true wisdom as something that must be shared orally, not written and read. This coincides still today with my experience as a pastor leading a small rural church where the people did not trust, as they said, "book learning," but only that which came from experience.

2. Craddock, *Preaching*, 167.

3. For preachers who do not prefer to write out a complete manuscript, this would be the part of the sermon process that results in the outline or arrangement of thoughts that will finally result in a delivered sermon.

4. Craddock, *Without Authority*. Others would follow, but Craddock really led the way in conceiving of the sermon in this way. The 1st ed. of this classic work was published in 1974.

traveler, during the preaching of the Word of God, and so today, as we continue building upon those insights, we must regard the listener as such. In the case of Law and Gospel preaching, the event in which we and the listener are engaged is the experience of being lost to being found, or being dead to being made alive, or being estranged to being reconciled, or whatever experience of the law and gospel the text provides for us. As I have emphasized, the task of the sermon will be to *do* in the sermon *what the Word does* in the text, as well as to do whatever law or gospel work must be accomplished in addition to what is done in the text. But no matter what the goal of the sermon, and no matter what approach is decided upon, the sermon must always be conceived of as *an event in time* in which the listener is a co-participant and not merely a passive spectator. This is crucial. It would perhaps be helpful now to look briefly at a few of the basic concepts the pioneers of the New Homiletic taught us and see how these ideas can help us shape our sermons as Law and Gospel preachers.[5]

Fred Craddock

We begin by considering the work of Fred Craddock, whose work informed all the rest. Craddock looked at the work of his predecessors in the homiletical field and concluded that they had not considered the listener a partner in the sermon, but rather had regarded the listener as simply a recipient of the truths the preacher announced. Craddock wondered why a more inductive approach might not work. He asked, "Why not on Sunday morning retrace the inductive trip [that the preacher has made earlier during the sermon preparation process] and see if the hearers come to that same conclusion?"[6] He argued that the power and effectiveness of the sermon would be heightened considerably for "if *they* [the

5. Allen, *Renewed Homiletic*. O. Wesley Allen cites these five gentlemen as the "pillars of the New Homiletic" who have transformed preaching in the last forty years. Certainly there are other teachers who have also made contributions, but I believe Allen is right in calling these the pioneers.

6. Craddock, *Without Authority*, 48.

listeners] have made the trip, it is *their* conclusion, and the implication for their own situations is not only clear but personally inescapable."[7]

What can be seen immediately is that this approach to preaching is precisely what is required in Law and Gospel preaching. The goal is always to bring the listener through an experience of being lost to being found. Therefore, any notion that we can do this deductively is suspect. In other words, a listener is not brought to his or her knees in repentance when we preach *about* the problem of "lostness." But, as Craddock said, let us speak about the recent suicide at the high school, or the alcoholism that robbed a young man of his health and livelihood, or the closing of the manufacturing plant in town, and suddenly lostness is not a sleepy concept but a reality that people recognize as present in their own lives. Likewise, when we preach *about* the idea of "being found," the congregation might nod [off!] in sleepy approval, but let us preach about the recent rescue of a drowning person at a nearby lake, or the successful mediation in a long, drawn-out strike, or the reconciliation of long-estranged family members, and suddenly being found is no longer a sleepy concept, but a reality in the listeners' lives. So in writing the sermon, we, as preachers of law and gospel are careful not to merely preach *about* being lost or being found, but rather are cognizant that our job as preacher is to bring our listeners into a place where the Word will do its work of showing them that indeed *they* "once were lost, but now [are] found, were blind but now [they] see." And this is done most effectively, as Craddock pointed out, not by announcing a principle and illustrating it with examples (what we might call the deductive method), but by mining the real life experiences of the listeners and then letting the listeners come to their own conclusions regarding their state

7. Ibid., 49. Craddock even went so far as to say that the deductive approach to preaching (i.e., reasoning from the general to the specific) would no longer work in America. "The inductive process is fundamental to the American way of life. There are now at least two generations who have been educated in this way from kindergarten through college. Experience figures prominently in the process, not just at the point of *receiving* lessons and truths to be implemented, but in the process of *arriving* at those truths."

of being lost or being found. This is what Craddock called "the inductive method."[8]

Craddock revolutionized the role of the preacher by actually inviting the listener to complete the sermon. He understood that this way of thinking about the sermon event put into motion an important Lutheran teaching: the doctrine of the priesthood of all believers. He placed some of the responsibility for meaning making into the hands of the listener and thereby honored each person who listened. He transformed the listener from passive audience to active participant in the sermon.[9] And the partial loss of control of meaning that resulted for the preacher was apparently no concern at all for Craddock, for he wrote: "The charge that every listener hears a different sermon is simply an unnerving fact with which we all have to live."[10]

So now let us look at a few examples of how this way of thinking might work itself out in our manuscript writing. John 11:32–44 is the gospel text appointed for All Saints Day, in the Year of Mark. In this text we have the dramatic conclusion of the story of the raising of Lazarus. In the story, the Word, Jesus, is calling into the tomb, "Lazurus, come out!" and the dead man comes out. Clearly the Word is working in this text to defeat death. The place of the listener could be in one of two places: either as one of the grieving sisters of the dead man, who witness this death and resurrection, or the dead man himself. Let us say that we have chosen the sisters as the identity for our listeners. Once we decide this we can

8. Reid, "Faithful Preaching," 169. Reid compares Karl Barth's approach to Craddock's, saying that Barth facilitated "an *encounter* with God and God's Word" and Craddock provided "the means for an individual to have an *experience of meaning* that centers or re-centers the life of faith."

9. Craddock, *Without Authority*, 53–59. Craddock wrote: "Participation of the hearer is essential, not just in the post-benediction implementation, but in the completion of the thought, movement and decision-making with the sermon itself. The process calls for an incompleteness, a lack of exhaustiveness in the sermon. It requires the preacher that she resist the temptation to tyranny of ideas rather than democratic sharing. She restrains herself, refusing to do both the speaking and listening, to give both stimulus and response, or in a more homely analogy, she does not throw the ball and catch it herself."

10. Ibid., 58.

identify the listeners' mindset; it is as the helpless mourners who say, "Lord, if you had been here, my brother would not have died." At the outset, then, in the law portion of the sermon, our job is to invite the listener into the mourner's position, perhaps by telling about a death in one's own family, or a recent death in the congregation, or some experience of death that is current in the media. The task, remember, is not to *describe* a mourner's position, but to invite the listeners to *experience* themselves as mourners. If we do this well, the listeners will hear the sermon and become mourners with Mary and Martha, grieving with them, and nodding as they feel the helplessness of watching a loved one die.

Similarly in the gospel portion of the sermon, we bring to bear the announcement that Jesus has defeated death. But instead of speaking *about* resurrection, we help the listeners *experience* it. This might be done by reciting the glorious words from the throne of God in the second reading for the day, Revelation 21:1–6a: "See the home of God is among mortals. He will dwell with them; they will be his peoples, and God himself will be with them; he will wipe every tear from their eyes. Death will be no more; mourning and crying and pain will be no more, for the first things have passed away." Of course, there are a number of other wonderful options (e.g., 1 Thess 5; 1 Cor 15; other texts from John's Revelation), including words from the first reading appointed for the day: "And he will destroy on this mountain the shroud that is cast over all peoples, the sheet that is spread over all nations; he will swallow up death forever" (Isa 25:7–8a). The task, remember, is to announce Christ's victory and to help the listeners *experience* that victory.

Another example could be the gospel appointed for the Seventeenth Sunday after Pentecost in the Year of Luke: Luke 15:1–10. The way the Word is working in this text is quite clear: The Word, God, is searching for and rescuing the lost. In this text the lost include the one lost sheep out in the wilderness and the lost coin for which the woman searches until she finds it. In both cases God is shown to be searching diligently to find the lost and then celebrating wildly when the lost is found. Similarly, in the remainder of the chapter, which is not a part of this pericope, when the lost son is found upon his return home, his father celebrates wildly. Knowing these things, then we are clear that the couplet that will be put into play in this sermon is being lost/being found. So to begin, again we help the listeners identify with the lost ones. We do not describe lostness in any great detail, but share stories or illustrations or experiences whereby our listeners are drawn into the position of saying, "I've been there. I know how that feels. I too have been lost. I am lost right now."

Then, in the move that is always crucial in the Law and Gospel sermon, Christ becomes present for the listener in the gospel portion of the sermon. In this case, we move into the mode of announcing how Christ has been searching for each one of us. We might point out to our listeners that they are in worship that morning precisely because Christ has been calling their name and seeking them out. We might describe our own experience of being found, or of some event in the media reporting the rescue of a victim of fire or flood, or any powerful experience of being rescued. Once again, we invite the listener into the *experience* of being rescued, or being found, and in hearing this, the listener is saved. Faith is born!

What I am attempting to illustrate in these two examples is Craddock's inductive method at work in a Law and Gospel sermon. This method always seeks to engage our listeners in an event in time whereby they experience first the law (you need Christ!) and then the gospel (here is Christ!). Much of Craddock's method is integral to the task.[11]

---

11. For a complete understanding of Craddock's method, one needs to go to the source and put into practice the principles of Craddock's classic *As One Without Authority*. Beyond that, every preacher should have a copy of the textbook Craddock developed to guide his students through this process of preaching, from start to finish. This text is entitled simply *Preaching*, first being published in 1985, fourteen years after he first began writing about the inductive method.

Charles Rice

The pioneer of the New Homiletic who perhaps most explicitly attributed his reorientation in preaching to Fred Craddock is Charles Rice, who in 1980, along with his colleagues Edmund Steimle and Morris Niedenthal, published *Preaching the Story*. In this work, these writers posited that the need was for the preacher to blend the four basic components of the preaching event: the preacher, the listener, the ecclesiastical and social context, and the message. Furthermore, they argued that they needed "to find that formative image that could both articulate what preaching is and free people to do it."[12] Finally they landed on the storyteller as the formative image that was up to this task, and they suggested that one could find no better definition of preaching than "shared story."[13]

Rice argued that sermon as shared story "makes a place for each of our stories to make contact with and to be integrated into the stories of the Bible and of other people."[14] Rice advised all preachers to share their life with their listeners, to be transparent to them, and to allow one's own story to be an integral part of the preaching. Along with the preacher's own story, Rice and his colleagues exhorted us to be conversant with the stories of our listeners. They suggested that in any time or place there is "a common Story, a shared Story [that] runs deep in peoples' lives, affecting profoundly the ways in which they feel and think and live."[15] They insisted that we must be able to tell this story in such a way that our listeners recognize this story as their own and thereby are drawn into a place where the gospel word can touch them. While these writers identified fear and anxiety as the "overpowering dynamics" of contemporary life in their day, and while today we might identify other issues as critical in understanding our context, no matter the era, these writers help us understand how important it is for us as preachers to tell the shared story of our listeners.

12. Steimle et al., *Preaching*, 11–12.
13. Ibid., 13.
14. Ibid., 34.
15. Ibid., 75.

The third component of preaching that these writers tackle is the ecclesiastical or liturgical culture into which the sermon is imbedded. They suggest that a "sensitive preacher will be able to weave into the sermon, almost in throwaway fashion, the images, phrases, words, and figures of the liturgy in order to strengthen the connections between the two."[16] I have often found this to be true as a sermon of mine might regularly call on the words of the confession and absolution, the words of institution from the Lord's Supper, or simply phrases from the Lord's Prayer, for example, to enhance the message. Of course, this assumes that the worship includes these liturgical elements and perhaps begs the question for those of us who have made the decision to leave much of the church's liturgy behind. In so doing could we not thereby be impoverishing our preaching by eliminating a resource of memory that would help our listeners connect their story with the church's story?

In the discussion of the fourth and final component of the preaching event, Rice and his colleagues, unlike the other pioneers of the New Homiletic, address directly the issue of Law and Gospel preaching. Morris Niedenthal, in his chapter entitled "The Irony and Grammar of the Gospel" goes to the heart of the matter when he talks about the difference between the grammar of the law and the grammar of the gospel. Niedenthal makes the following observations about the grammar of the law:

1. The future is made to depend entirely upon the past (i.e., if you repent, you will be forgiven).

2. It is safe and simplistic. If the future promise does not materialize, it is of course because the condition was not properly met.

3. It presupposes strength but does nothing to create it.[17]

The gospel, on the other hand, has a completely opposite grammar:

16. Ibid., 99.
17. Ibid., 147–48.

1. The grammar of the gospel opens a new and different future by declaring an action of God that alters the meaning of the past.

2. The grammar of the gospel does not presuppose strength but seeks to create it by ministering to its needs and weaknesses.[18]

It seems to me that this distinction between law and gospel, made obvious by talking in terms of their "grammar" is a very helpful way of thinking about the task of Law and Gospel preaching as we go forward. It would be a good check for preachers to refer occasionally to Niedenthal's criteria and see whether our grammar matches our intent as we make the distinction between law and gospel in our preaching.

Eugene Lowry

Another of the early followers of Craddock was Eugene Lowry, whose book *The Homiletical Plot* was also published in 1980. In this book Lowry argued that the task of the preacher in developing a sermon was "not to assemble parts, but to facilitate a process."[19] Lowry suggested that we think of our task as preachers as if we were playwrights, hence his choice of the title *The Homiletical Plot*. Lowry said that the preacher's task was to set the listener in the middle of an issue that demanded some kind of resolution. Lowry called this issue the "homiletical bind," and he argued that this "sensed discrepancy" was a key ingredient of any sermon. Quoting the work of Lutheran teacher, Robert Roth, he said, "Meaning [for the listener] arises from the experience of personal involvement in the dramatic action."[20] Lowry achieved this dramatic action by inventing a sermon form in which the listener was taken on a journey from equilibrium to disequilibrium and back again. Interestingly, it was Lowry's students at Saint Paul School of Theology in Kansas City, Missouri, who came up with a shorthand way of

18. Ibid., 149.

19. Lowry, *Homiletical Plot*, 14.

20. Ibid., 15. Lowry quotes from Roth, *Story and Reality*, 38.

remembering the five stages of this journey: "(1) Oops, (2) Ugh, (3) Aha, (4) Whee, and (5) Yeah."[21]

In stage one of Lowry's form, the listener's equilibrium is upset (Oops). Lowry says that in the first two to three minutes we must "provide clues as to the issue at stake and the difficulties of sorting out the ingredients—even the apparent unlikelihood of resolving the matter."[22] In stage two "the discrepancy is analyzed."[23] During this stage our listeners are sent even deeper into the matter that has been introduced in the first stage, hence their sense of disequilibrium deepens (Ugh). Stage three, the "Aha" moment of the sermon, is the point at which we disclose the clue to the resolution of the issue. This clue serves to "reverse the underlying assumption" of our listener.[24] In the example that Lowry gives, the preacher seems to be preaching about how one can find oneself, but then discovers that the key to finding oneself is understanding oneself as one who is found by God. This "process of reversal" is a key move for Lowry.[25] The fourth stage is when the listener truly experiences the gospel (Whee). Lowry writes: "Stages one, two, and three are intended to prepare the way so that when the gospel is then proclaimed it is *effective*—that is, it *does* what it says, and is that to which it refers."[26] (Doesn't that sound familiar!) Finally, in stage five new doors are opened as our listeners are invited to see how life can now be lived in light of the gospel. This stage, called "anticipating the consequences," his students called "Yeah."[27] Again, this sounds uncannily like Stuempfle's "call to obedience" and indeed it has the same function, helping the listener think about what life might look like once Christ has made all things new.[28]

21. Ibid., 25.
22. Ibid., 35.
23. Ibid., 36.
24. Ibid., 53.
25. Ibid., 56.
26. Ibid., 64.
27. Ibid., 67.
28. As with Craddock's book, I would recommend that any preacher read

Lowry's method is fleshed out even further in a later work, *The Sermon: Dancing the Edge of Mystery*, published in 1997. In this work Lowry suggests the multiple ways that disequilibrium can be achieved when we use different sermon forms, such as the story sermon, the inductive sermon, the episodal sermon, the narrative sermon, or the transconscious African American sermon.[29] He also does an excellent job of showing how careful we must be in letting the text guide the actual stages of the sermon. In a very careful way he shows that the shift to the gospel may come at very different points in the sermon, depending on the text, with the good news (the Aha/Whee) announced in some cases in the middle of the sermon and in other cases, near the end of the sermon.[30] Lowry says, "What is important is the preacher's concentration in preparation not on the final naming of the good news, but on the search for the sudden shift. Once found, it will by its nature 'tell' the preacher whether it should come before, at, or after the good news."[31] Lowry reminds us again of how we "dance on the edge of mystery" in writing a sermon. There is no set formula, no sure-fire sequence, no tried and true method of fashioning a sermon that will guarantee our listeners' experience of the gospel. The text guides us, and the Holy Spirit has its way with us and our listeners, and we are, as Lowry likes to say, merely midwives at a birth.[32]

One can see in Lowry's method much that immediately dovetails with our concerns as Law and Gospel preachers. First of all, Lowry's call to introduce a "discrepancy" or an unsettling notion into the minds of our listeners is precisely the function of the law in any Law and Gospel sermon. Similarly, the second stage of Lowry's method, which deepens the disequilibrium of our listeners, is precisely the effect that the law has upon listeners. In the simple definition of the law that I suggested earlier, the law says, "You

---

for her or himself *The Homiletical Plot* in order to appreciate the nuances of this excellent approach.

29. Lowry, *Dancing*, 70–74.

30. Ibid., 81–85.

31. Ibid., 84.

32. Ibid., 53.

need Christ," and indeed this is akin to the sense of disequilibrium that Lowry talks about.

It can also be seen that Lowry's method connects very well with the Crossing Community's notion of the effect of the law. The Crossings Method, you recall (see diagram on page 39), suggests that we begin by pointing out the "bad fruits" that grow out of the kind of lostness that the text is lifting up (D1). In the second stage of the Crossings Method (D2), our task is to deepen this sense of lostness by pointing out the false gods that our listeners may be trusting in which cause these bad fruits to grow. This, it seems to me, is very close to Lowry's second stage in which the discrepancy is analyzed. The Crossings Method goes one step further, of course, by deepening the sense of lostness in a third stage called Diagnosis 3 (D3), where our listeners are confronted with our estrangement from God as a result of our sin. We would have to assume that Lowry's method could also accommodate this, but this third stage of the law (D3) would be included in the second stage of Lowry's form.

Stage three (Aha) and stage four (Whee) of Lowry's method are where the gospel is brought to bear, although the third stage serves only as the platform for the announcement of the gospel, as it serves only to begin the "reversal process" in the listener's thinking. In the Crossings Method, there is an equivalent stage: the presentation of Christ's work in the fourth stage (P4). The difference here is that in P4 the gospel is not merely hinted at, but it is presented in all of its power as the person and work of Jesus Christ is brought front and center. The fifth and sixth stages of the Crossings Method provide the place where the results of Christ's work are shown in the listener's life. In stage five (P5), we announce how Christ changes our hearts to trust in the true God. Then in stage six (P6), we show how this new trust in the living God shows itself in bearing good fruit. Both of these final stages in the Crossings Method could be understood as achieving what Lowry hopes to achieve in his final stage (Yeah), for Lowry's final stage is our chance to show what life might be like in light of Christ's work in our lives. This is precisely what the Crossing Method calls "good fruits."

We might diagram the parallel structure of Lowry's method with the Crossings Method structure in the following way:

	Law			Gospel		
Crossings Method	D1	D2	D3	P4	P5	P6
Lowry Method	Oops	Ugh	Ugh	Aha/ Whee	Yeah	

Having seen how Lowry's method can be brought to bear on an established law/gospel form, let us look at a couple of examples of sermons that use this method and see if we can understand how this might work in actual practice.

Mark 1:9–15 is the gospel text appointed for the First Sunday in Lent in the Year of Mark. In this text we have the familiar story of Jesus' time of temptation in the wilderness following his baptism, albeit in Mark the description of his wilderness time is only one verse long. In Mark's brief version of this story Jesus is *driven* by the Spirit into the wilderness, unlike the versions in Matthew and Luke where the more benign verb *led* is used. Because the Word—in this text, the Spirit—is functioning to drive the Son of God into the wilderness, one tack we might take is to identify our listeners as children of God who may be, similarly, at times driven into a place far from their comfort zone. We could begin by giving examples or telling a story of being forced out of our own comfort zone by those who love us. We could suggest that it is counterintuitive for us that someone who loves us would "drive us into the wilderness," but perhaps that is exactly what we need. In so doing we would be achieving the disequilibrium that Lowry points out is essential for the sermon. We could deepen this disequilibrium by giving examples of how comfort zones can actually be "dead zones." That is to say, comfort zones can be places where we are not stretched, not used by God in any significant way, and thus we begin to lose our way: We "get lost" even while we are in our comfort/ dead zones. This would be the Ugh stage of the sermon. Finally, in a move that the Crossings Method would suggest, we could also illustrate how these dead zones are graves for us spiritually, where finally we are estranged from God (D3). The reversal in Lowry's method comes with the announcement that precisely in the place where we least expect it—the wilderness!—we encounter Christ. Christ too has been driven into the wilderness, out of his comfort zone, and much to our surprise, Christ has been driven into *our* wilderness, precisely to seek *us* out. Upon meeting Christ in our wilderness we suddenly understand something that we never would have known had we not been driven there—that the wilderness is a place where God is still totally present. In this move are clearly the Aha and Whee stages of Lowry's method (P4), whereby our listeners experience the gospel. But then we could deepen this gospel word by reminding our listeners that the wilderness has always been the place where God's people have gone to be formed into the people of God (P5). Think of Israel at Sinai, think of the exiles in Babylon, think of the persecuted believers in the book of Acts; they have all been driven into "the wilderness" and there have become God's people. And as God's people have understood that God drives the baptized children of God into the wilderness to be formed into the community of faith, then they too can begin to venture outside their comfort zone to the wilderness places of others, and do the work they are called to do. This finally is Lowry's Yeah (P6) as our listeners gain insight into what it means to live as wilderness people, and celebrate that identity.

Another example illustrating these two methods at work could be the readings appointed for the Twelfth Sunday after Pentecost in the Year of Luke: Genesis 15:1–6; Hebrews 11:1–3, 8–16; and Luke 12:32–40. In these three texts we have the Word—here, Jesus—encouraging folks to live by faith in things which are unseen, and believe that God will be with them: "Do not be afraid little flock, for it is your Father's good pleasure to give you the kingdom." We might begin by pointing out the many ways in which we are easily seduced into believing that the visible world is the only reality worth attending to. We might point out the beauty of creation, the wonder of a child's birth, or the amazing complexity of the human mind, and show how easy it is to be drawn into believing that what we see is all there is (D1/Oops). Then we might deepen this problem by reminding our listeners that everything we see will pass away: our friends, our families, our homes, our possessions, indeed this entire world (D2/Ugh). Finally, we might remind our listeners that God is unseen, and to give ourselves completely over to what is seen is to go down a path that eventually will lead us far away from the Unseen One who has created us and all that exists (D3/Ugh). The reversal comes when we make it clear that God, in God's amazing compassion and mercy, knows that we are bound to the visible, but instead of condemning us for this, sends the Son, so that we who are bound to the visible can see God (P4/Aha). As Jesus himself says, "Whoever has seen me has seen the Father" (John 14:9). This Son then not only shows us the Father, but tells us the amazing news that it is "the Father's pleasure to give [us] the kingdom" (P4/Whee). Hearing this, faith is born in us, and we are released from our grasping after all things visible. We begin to live by faith and not by sight, and the freedom that comes to us brings with it great joy (P5). Finally, living in this joy, we are not afraid to live our lives generously and boldly, not grasping all things to ourselves, but sharing freely with others what we have, confident that it is truly the Father's good pleasure to give us the kingdom (P6/Yeah).

David Buttrick

The pioneer of the New Homiletic who came along a bit later in its development was David Buttrick, professor of homiletics and worship at Vanderbilt Divinity School in Nashville. In 1987 he published a large work called *Moves and Structures* wherein he explored "how sermons happen in consciousness."[33] For this reason, his work has been called "phenomenological" as he attempts to understand "what may actually take place in consciousness during the production and hearing of the sermon."[34] In simplest terms,

33. Buttrick, *Moves*, xii.
34. Ibid.

Buttrick's main thesis is that sermons are always made up of a series of rhetorical units or moves, and these moves are tied together by various "natural logics" into structures.[35] He suggests that all human speech is organized in this way, but in the case of a sermon, the pace at which these moves may be presented is really quite deliberate. He says that in the space of a twenty-minute sermon we can hope to present no more than six different moves—probably better kept to five—if we expect our listeners to stay the course. Buttrick reminds us that each move must be "oriented, imaged and explained," thus it takes some time to develop each move.[36] Buttrick also writes about our need to strategize the presentation of each move in order to overcome opposition and keep our listeners on track.[37] "What makes a good sermon," says Buttrick, "is not one single illustration, but a gridwork of interacting images, examples, and illustrations."[38] Also, Buttrick offers a basic test of any structure the preacher sets up. He asks the following questions:

"(1) Does one phrase follow another 'naturally' without strain or non sequitur? (2) Are all phrases simple, non-compound sentences (except with narrative passages)? (3) When read aloud does the entire sequence seem to come together in consciousness and make meaning?"[39]

If any of these three conditions are not met, he advises the preacher to go back and try again.

Buttrick's insights into the consciousness of the preacher and the listener match well with what we have been exploring in the Law and Gospel sermon. In the forms of Law and Gospel preaching we have explored there is an inherent structure that moves the listener logically from one place to the next. There are "natural

35. Ibid., 24.

36. Ibid., 26.

37. Ibid., 34. Much of Buttrick's work is composed of giving advice on strategies such as how to write introductions and conclusions, and the use of images and illustrations. There are some terrific tips here for any aspiring preacher. The book is well worth the expense for the preacher who wishes to expand her or his "tool kit."

38. Ibid., 153.

39. Ibid., 312.

logics" that tie together the moves from the opening of the sermon where the need of the listener is exposed, through the climax when the work of Christ is announced, to the conclusion where the listener is given some hint as to what this new life in Christ might look like. In simple terms a Law and Gospel sermon is a Buttrick-like structure of moves that lead listeners to despair of their own ability to save themselves and then long for the salvation that Christ alone can bring. It seems to me that Buttrick's work gives any Law and Gospel preacher an abundance of good advice on how to best proceed in structuring a sermon that will flow logically and adhere together well in the listener's consciousness.

Henry Mitchell

Another pioneer, Henry Mitchell, whose first work *The Recovery of Preaching* came out at nearly the same time as Fred Craddock's first work, is mostly remembered for his later book *Celebration and Experience in Preaching* that was published about the same time as Buttrick's *Moves and Structures*. Mitchell very much recognizes Buttrick's influence in his own thinking.[40] Both writers are interested in how consciousness forms in a listener's mind, and they are agreed that the sermon must include certain defined "moves" if it is to attain its goal.

As the title of his work indicates, Mitchell believes that experience and celebration are essential pieces in influencing a listener's response to a sermon. He asks, "What methods are best used of God to 'over-record' or replace the tapes of childhood terrors and distrust, and otherwise strengthen the tapes of trust?" He replies, "The answer . . . is *experiential encounter*."[41] By experiential encounter he means "a homiletical plan in which the aim is to offer direct or vicarious encounters with and experiences of truths already fully certified as biblical, coherent, and relevant."[42] And he

---

40. Mitchell, *Celebration*, 50.

41. Ibid., 25.

42. Ibid., 25.

goes on to say that such encounters are very important resources "by which God moves to create the miracle of faith."[43]

Mitchell is highly skeptical of any claim that an appeal to mere intellect can move any listener to faith in God or faithfulness to the God of Scripture. He says that any preacher who preaches without emotion has not "faced squarely the emotional character of faith and hope and love."[44] He points out that educators have long known that "what we celebrate (get emotional about) we retain far longer."[45]

Mitchell spends considerable time, as Buttrick does in his book, giving practical advice on how to create an "experiential encounter."[46] He also is very concerned that we understand that the goal of a sermon is not simply to get a point across but to change behavior. (This is much like Craddock's maxim that the point is not merely to get something *said* but to get something *heard*.) Mitchell says, "The goal of each move within the sermon is to help the gospel to form in consciousness."[47] And finally, he reminds us that if the gospel is good news *it is worth celebrating*. He berates any preacher who uses the pulpit to beat down the people of God, and instead insists that "celebration is the best way to motivate people to *do* the will of God."[48]

It seems to me that what Mitchell does is to take Buttrick's idea of moves and structures and add another dimension to it. His appeal, coming out of the African American tradition of preaching, is for us to enter into the gospel portion of the Law and Gospel sermon and "let it all hang out." He says that heightened rhetoric,

43. Ibid., 80.

44. Ibid., 29.

45. Ibid., 30.

46. Ibid., 37–47. In this chapter Mitchell introduces his seven "genres" by which a preacher may present a text: Narrative; Character Sketch; Group Study; Dialogue; Monologue or Testimony; Metaphor, Simile and Analogs; and Stream of Consciousness. The second half of the book is devoted entirely to a detailed explanation of each of these genres and how they might be incorporated into the sermon. This is an excellent resource for any preacher.

47. Ibid., 58.

48. Ibid., 63.

poetic license, and hyperbole are all *indispensable* when we are preaching in the mode of celebration.[49] For Mitchell there are no holds barred as he exhorts us to leave our decorum behind and be the first person in the congregation to wade into "the waters of ecstasy."[50] This, I must admit, is a challenge for this Scandinavian Lutheran, but I hear Mitchell's exhortation and agree that we are often far too timid in our announcement of God's victory in Christ. Why not take Lowry's Aha/Whee/Yeah and really put an exclamation point on those stages of gospel presentation? Let us hear Mitchell's challenge and strive to truly celebrate the good news whenever we have opportunity!

49. Ibid., 67.
50. Ibid., 68.

5

Law and Gospel: A Methodology

THIS BOOK IS NOT meant to be an exhaustive review of the homiletical literature nor is it an attempt to suggest all the ways we may proceed when moving through the sermon process. There is a host of fine books on many subjects from exegesis to delivery that I have found helpful, and I urge any serious preacher to attend preaching workshops, subscribe to preaching journals, and quiz colleagues to learn all she or he can about what resources might be most helpful in one's quest to become a preacher of excellence.[1]

Even after much study and practice, preaching remains for me a challenging, frustrating, and exhilarating experience that eludes my grasp at mastery. I expect it will remain so. I do hope that what is clear is that I have been attempting to synthesize the insights of Law and Gospel theologians with those of the chief proponents of the New Homiletic movement that began with Fred Craddock's work in the 1970s.[2] This is both a quest of my own and an attempt

1. If a person is interested in a sweeping review of the homiletical literature, especially as it relates to Law and Gospel preaching, one can do no better than Paul Scott Wilson's *Preaching and Homiletical Theory*. Other works I have found especially helpful are: Long, *Preaching and Literary Forms of the Bible*; Troeger, *Imagining a Sermon* and *Ten Strategies for Preaching in a Multi-Media Culture*; Childers, *Performing the Word*; Schlafer, *Your Way with God's Word*; Black, *Healing Homiletic*.

2. I suppose we could even give credit to Thor Hall, who in the 1970

to respond to the challenge posed by O. Wesley Allen when he stated in his 2010 review of the New Homiletic that "many people are looking for the next major move in preaching," but noting that "it is not likely that such a move will be an abandonment of the New Homiletic so much as it will be an extension and adaptation of it."[3] Also, I note David Buttrick's comment in that same work that "somehow we must recover theology" in our preaching through our "tinkering with the New Homiletic." He writes:

> If theology is gone, then people have nothing left with which to interpret life but their own social commitments. They are Republicans, or Masons, or black, or gay, or Democrats, southern or northern, hawks or pacifists, or just flag-waving All-Americans. What's more, they interpret the Bible from these same social commitments. Maybe we will have to stop handing out therapies and teach our congregations how to think theologically all over again. Somehow our preaching must help to restore a theological awareness to the American mind.[4]

I believe that the merger of Law and Gospel theology with New Homiletic thinking can restore this theological awareness to preaching, and I believe it might also be at least a partial response to Allen's challenge. I believe that what I have laid out here is a methodology—a way of thinking—that can be very helpful to any preacher who is attempting to both preach to contemporary listeners and retain an awareness of what is at stake theologically in any text they encounter.

But, as the old saying goes, the proof of the pudding is in the eating—so let us now take a number of texts and apply the method that has been suggested in the preceding pages and see how well it succeeds in leading us to a sermon worth preaching. First, I will present a sermon from its inception: exegesis to full manuscript.

James Sprunt Lectures at Union Theological Seminary in Richmond, Virginia, issued the call for the "new homiletic" to which Craddock responded. See Hall, *Future Shape of Preaching*, xviii.

3. Allen, *Renewed Homiletic*, 18.

4. Ibid., 110–11.

Then, in the second example, I will present the full manuscript first and follow it with the exegetical and methodological analysis.

Sermon Example 1—A Reformation Day Sermon: "Insulted by Christ?"

Since I am a diehard Lutheran I begin with the texts appointed for Reformation Sunday. In the Revised Common Lectionary they are the same every year: Jeremiah 31:31–34, Romans 3:19–28, and John 8:31–36.

How Does the Word Function?

The first question is: "How does the Word function in each of these texts?" We could summarize it as follows:

Jer 31:31–34—Establishment of a new covenant is announced

Rom 3:19–28—Announcement that all are justified by grace, apart from works

John 8:31–36—Insistence that no one is free apart from the Son

Seeing the function of these texts in this way, the first thing we might notice is how offensive each of these texts could be to its listeners. The hearers of Jeremiah's announcement might well say, "We don't need a new covenant; the old one is fine for us." They might also have taken offense at the statement (in v. 32) that their ancestors broke the first covenant. Similarly in the Romans passage, an early hearer might have protested, "*All* of us are justified by grace? Certainly there are *some* who are righteous." Just as likely, the listener might well have taken offense when Paul insisted that "*all* have sinned and fallen short of the glory of God." Finally in John's gospel the offense to the hearers is clear. When Jesus insists "the truth will make you free" they say, "We are descendants of Abraham and have never been slaves to anyone. What do you mean by saying, 'You will be made free'?" What is explicit in the John text, but could be inferred in the other two texts, is that the

Word is functioning to insult the listeners. Indeed if we look at the surrounding verses in John 8 we see over and over that Jesus is insulting and infuriating his listeners:

Verses 23–24: "You are from below, I am from above; you are of this world, I am not of this world. I told you that you would die in your sins, for you will die in your sins unless you believe that I am he."

Verse 44: "You are from your father the devil, and you choose to do your father's desires. He was a murderer from the beginning and does not stand in the truth, because there is no truth in him."

Verses 58–59: "Jesus said to them, 'Very truly, I tell you, before Abraham was, I am.' So they picked up stones to throw at him, but Jesus hid himself and went out of the temple."

This function of the Word is very important for us here, because it demands a tricky thing: We must, at some level, insult our listeners! Of course, we are not called upon here to insult them for any reason we choose, but rather to insult them precisely as the Word does, by pointing out to them that they are not free, even though they claim to be. This is a task worthy of all the skill and craft any of us can muster!

With Whom Are We Identifying in the Text?

At this point it is also important to take note with whom we preachers, and therefore our listeners, are identifying with in these texts. It is always important to identify with the people who are addressed by the Word, yet particularly in this text, it is very tempting for us to want to identify with Jesus or Paul or the prophet. We might think that we would never be among those who would be insulted by the words of Jesus. We should know better. We are just as likely as the people of Israel to chafe at the notion that our ancestors were in any way unfaithful, or that there are none who are righteous, or that we are not free. If we assume any of these stances we are likely to become condescending haranguers who only end up beating down our listeners, reminding them that they are unfaithful, unrighteous, and in bondage, but failing completely to see this as true for ourselves! This is why it is so important to identify with those whom the Word addresses.

How Is the Word Not Functioning in the Text?

Once we see clearly how the Word is functioning in the text, we must also be very clear as to how the Word is *not* functioning. Often a text functions only as one or the other, law or gospel, not both. In these texts, however, we actually have an example of both law and gospel at work. In Jeremiah we have the announcement that the old covenant has been broken (law), but that God is establishing a new one (gospel). In the Romans text we see Paul reminding us that all have sinned and fallen short of God's glory (law), but that all are now justified by God as a gift (gospel). And in John we have Jesus announcing that "everyone who commits sin is a slave to sin" (law), but "if the Son makes you free, you will be free indeed" (gospel).

In these texts it is clear when the law and gospel are at work; when it is the law at work, *we* are the subject of the action, and when the gospel is at work, *God* is the subject. With these Reformation texts, then, one can see that it will not be necessary for the preacher to depart from the appointed texts in order to fulfill the requirement to preach *both* law and gospel; they are both present in all the pericopes.

The Call to Obedience

The final piece of initial analysis concerns the "call to obedience." We need to ask, "What, if any call to discipleship is here, in these texts?" We must search the lessons and discern whether or not any implications for Christian living or Christian formation are present. If they are not, then it will be necessary for us to add this to the sermon for the day. In looking at these texts for Reformation Sunday it does not look to me like the call to obedience is present, therefore that will be a task that we will undertake as the sermon takes shape.

Exegetical Work

Having completed our initial analysis, it is our task to begin the hard work of looking carefully at the details of the text. We have many tools at our disposal: translation, word studies, commentaries, online blogs, concordances, and the like. The main thing is to ask as many questions of the text as possible, from as many different perspectives as possible.

If we look at the chapters surrounding the John text we see that this snippet from the middle of John 8 is part of an extensive controversy narrative between Jesus and the Jewish religious leaders. It might be helpful, therefore, to take on the role of one of these religious leaders and read the texts in first person, from their point of view. This might enable us to get a sense of the rage that they were experiencing at Jesus' words. Another thing to note is that *all* were not outraged at Jesus' words. Verse 30 says "many believed in him." So we see that the context of the text is important.

Another way to get at the meaning of a text is to read it in a number of different translations. In this text it is interesting to see how verse 33 is translated. In the King James Version we hear the leaders say that they "were never *in bondage* to any man." In the New International Version they say they have "never *been slaves* of anyone." The New English Bible translates the same verse, "never been *in slavery* to any man." The nuances of these translations might bring to mind insights that can be fruitful.

An essential exercise for me as an exegete is the translation of the text from its original language. If you are a seminarian, I would urge you to devote yourself to your Hebrew and Greek language study, for as my father memorably said, "There is no better commentary on the New Testament than the Greek Bible." I have found this to be so. One example of this is the presence of a conditional phrase in John 8:31: "If you continue in my word, you are truly my disciples." From Greek study we know that there are three types of conditional phrases: condition of fact, condition of contrary-to-fact, and condition of uncertainty. The English translation does not always give us a clear idea and today's lesson is a good example of that. Is Jesus saying, "If you continue in my word (and you are)"; or is he saying, "If you continue in my word (and you aren't)"; or is he saying, "If you continue in my word (and you might be or might not be)"? By translating from the Greek we can see that in this text we have a condition of uncertainty. That means that Jesus is saying, "If you continue in my word (and you might be or might not be), you are truly my disciples." Or we might translate the condition of uncertainty another way: "*Whenever* you continue in my word, you are truly my disciples." This, as you can see, can give us important insights into the text. Translation is often an excellent tool for getting at the details of a text's underlying meaning.

Word studies are another useful way of delving into the details of a text, and this John text is an excellent example of that. Kittel's *Theological Dictionary of the New Testament* has an extensive article on the meaning of freedom in the New Testament that is very helpful in this text.[5] Near the end of that article Kittel writes: "By the Spirit and power of the life of Jesus Christ radically offered up in love, there is brought into being in our lives an existence which is unselfish and self-forgetting because it is dynamically hidden in love and can no longer be self-seeking or self-willed. In the Spirit of the freedom of Jesus Christ, there arises our freedom."[6]

Commentaries also are often helpful in giving insights into a text, particularly theological commentaries that get at the heart of the matter. For example in the *Ancient Christian Commentary on Scripture* we find these words of Augustine in reference to this text:

"Our freedom comes when we subject ourselves to the truth."[7]

"In whatever measure we serve God, we are free. In whatever measure we serve the law of sin, we are still in bondage."[8]

5. Kittel, *TDNT*, 2:487–502.
6. Ibid., 2:499.
7. Oden, *ACCS*, New Testament, IVa, 296.
8. Ibid., 298.

Luther's commentary on the Gospel of John also is helpful: "Anything that is not God's Son will not make us free."[9]

"How, then, can I become free? Men answer: 'I will [do all this] . . .' But Christ says, '. . . No, let Him who is called the Son of God deliver you from sin; then you are free. If you give yourself to Him and let Him set you free, all is well.'"[10]

Another excellent commentary on John's gospel is Raymond Brown's classic work.[11] Some of Brown's insights include the following:

"Justin charges that the Jews, as seed of Abraham, expected to receive the kingdom of God no matter what their personal lives had become."[12]

"Jesus is saying to Jewish Christians that 'abiding in his word' is what distinguishes a true disciple."[13]

"[Freedom from sin is] the freedom of a true descendant of Abraham, [coming] only through the Son."[14]

There are many commentaries, both in book form and online that may be helpful to the preacher. These are just a few examples of things that have proved helpful to me with this text from John. The main task of exegesis is to ask questions, search for insights until that "eureka moment" comes when we gain a clear sense of what the text is saying. Once that moment comes, then, *and only then*, is the preacher ready to ask the second question, "How can I now *say* what the text says?" or, in law/gospel parlance, "How can I now best *do* what the text does?"

9. Pelikan, *Sermons on the Gospel of St. John*, 409.

10. Ibid., 413.

11. Brown, *Gospel according to John I–XII*.

12. Ibid., 361.

13. Ibid., 362.

14. Ibid., 363.

The Law/Gospel Couplet

The answer to the second question, "How can I now say what the text says?" begins with a decision as to how to structure the law/gospel couplet. As explained in chapter 3, we have a variety of models from which to choose, but in this case the couplet is laid out for us: bondage versus freedom. Nothing could be clearer. In the law portion of the sermon we are going to unveil the forms of bondage that we suffer, and in the gospel portion of the sermon we are going to announce to our listeners their freedom in Christ. Having said this, however, remember Stuempfle's word of caution that a Law and Gospel design is not simply a mechanism we can plug into our sermon and somehow out will come an effective sermon. A sermon is always a dynamic, living, developing entity that will come to life in its own way and in its own time according to the Spirit's leading. In other words, beware of thinking too mechanically about the Law and Gospel design.

Crossings Method

Before we get too far along in the design process, it would be helpful to look at whether or not a text lends itself to the Crossings Method. Sometimes I have found this method an excellent model to follow in designing a sermon. If we look online at the Crossings website, we can see that the texts appointed for each week in the cycle of the Revised Common Lectionary are archived and for each text there are a number of suggested Crossings examples. I have found that some of these examples work well and some not so well, so I advise being selective in including the Crossings Method in the sermon design for every sermon. Having said that, it is often thought-provoking to see what the Crossings Community has suggested for a particular text, regardless of whether we use it or not.

For John 8:31–36, the gospel appointed for Reformation Sunday, we see there are a number of suggestions. An analysis by Michael Hoy for Reformation Sunday 2010 produced the following design:

D1 *Protesting the Truth*: "We are descendants of Abraham . . . What do you mean 'you will be made free'?"

D2 *Slaves*: "We're not really interested in all this religion stuff."

D3 *No Permanent Place*: "What we 'have' is no lasting place."

P4 *Placed in Our No Place*: "But God knows this lack of permanence well. In fact, God experienced it first hand in Jesus."

P5 *Children*: "We become God's own kids. Hope starts to emerge."

P6 *Professing the Faith*: "I can trust this One, after all, because he knows my no-place."

As is typical with the Crossings Method, the strength of the design is its insistence that Christ's work be central, in this case the fact that Christ is "placed in our no place." The weakness of this particular example is that the call to obedience (P6) is not nearly as clear here as it often is in the Crossings Method.

In another analysis by Bruce T. Martin for Reformation Sunday 2013 we have the following:

D1 *Children of God? In-deed Not!*: "We are slaves to sin by what we do in-*deed*."

D2 *Slaves to Sin*: "We would rather trust our own word than Jesus' word."

D3 *Death*: "We slaves may be excluded at any time from the Father's household."

P4 *Life In-deed* or *Losing Us to Death*: "The Son makes us free by his life—indeed; that is, by his dying in our stead for our sin."

P5 *Receiving Jesus' Word*: "Faith is wholly receptive to Jesus and leans on Jesus."

P6 *Celebrating Jesus' Life In-deed*: "Faith is 'love' towards God and toward one another."[15]

---

15. By going to the Crossings Community website (www.crossings.org) you can view any of a number of sermon designs archived by lectionary text for all the years this community has produced them (1996 to present).

This analysis is, in my view, more balanced than the previous one since D2 exposes our willful disregard for Christ's word, and P5 announces the new faith in Christ's word that comes to us following the announcement of the gospel in P4. Also, the call to obedience (P6) is clearer in this design—our faith is translated into acts of love towards God and toward one another.

Writing the Sermon

By going through the above steps, we will have a clear idea not only of what the text is saying, but also of how we will say what the text is saying. In short, the sermon that has been growing in the womb during this process will now begin to show signs of wanting to be born. At this point, we are finally ready to write. The first thing we will write is the central theme and task of the sermon based on John 8:31–36. This is done to ensure that we have a clear focus at the outset, to avoid the ramblings that often result from an unfocused sermon design. In this sermon the central theme is "Christ's words offend *and* free us," and the central task is "to reveal our bondage *and* proclaim Christ's power over that bondage."

Dear Friends in Christ,

It was a long time ago now, but you know how *certain things just stick with you*. It was the day of my interviews with the bishops in Region 8, in order to receive my first call. I had been summoned to Philadelphia for the interviews, and on this particular day I met with the bishops from New England, upstate New York, and metro New York.

I sat down with a certain bishop who shall remain nameless, and he began immediately to grill me. "I see you're from the Midwest. Why do you want to serve out here? I see you went to Luther Seminary. I don't care much for what they teach you there." And on and on he went, pretty much trashing everything that had to do with my education, my background, and my theology. It wasn't exactly a pleasant time.

Then he stopped me dead in my tracks: "So, . . . do you have any issues with race?" "What?" I said. "Don't give me that. I mean are you a prejudiced person?" I was stunned.

Exactly how do you answer that? Should I say, "Well, I suppose I am, isn't everybody?" That probably wouldn't be the answer he was looking for. So I said, "Like anyone I suppose I have my issues, but so far as I know I'm not a *severely* prejudiced person." "Just as I suspected," he snorted, "You have no idea what's even *true* about yourself." And that was the end of the interview. Needless to say, my first call was not in the synod in which he served.

I left that interview that day, just aghast. Insulted! I mean, what kind of a question was that? "Are you a prejudiced person?"

He might as well have said, "So, have you ever eaten so much you got to feeling sick? Have you ever gone to a New Year's Eve party and gotten drunk? Have you ever had any thoughts and fantasies you shouldn't have? Have you ever been so angry you could have hurt someone?"

Why didn't he just go ahead and ask me *all* of those things? I mean, I'm a human being. I'm a sinner. What did he expect me to say!

I should have just answered, "Look, I'm captive to sin and cannot free myself, so shoot me."

I felt like the guy in that old Far Side cartoon where he comes out of the men's room and the neon sign above the door is buzzing and blinking in large letters, "Didn't wash his hands"!

It's a bummer being exposed as a sinner, isn't it?

It's not exactly a wonderful thing to have to confess, as we did today, "We have not loved you, O God, with our whole heart; we have not loved our neighbors as ourselves. Have mercy on us."

It's like a friend of mine says, "I don't like to confess I'm a sinner any more than I like those words we say on Ash Wednesday, 'You are dust, and to dust you shall return,' . . . but *they're both true.*"

Those Jewish disciples of Jesus who Jesus was disputing with in the gospel lesson for today didn't like the truth either. "What do you mean by saying, 'You will be made free?' We are descendants of Abraham and have never been slaves to anyone," they boasted.

Really? Never been slaves?

Had they forgotten about their ancestors' four hundred years of slavery in Egypt? Had they forgotten their exile in Babylon? Had they forgotten that even as they spoke Israel was occupied by the Roman army?

If we look back in the Old Testament only briefly we can see that part of the Hebrew statement of faith—the Hebrew Creed—included the words: I am the Lord your God, who brought you out of Egypt, *out of the house of bondage*; you shall have no other gods before me.

Had they forgotten that?

No, I don't suppose they had forgotten; I think that they, like us, just didn't want to think about it too much.

But Jesus was in no mood to soft-pedal their condition, and he is in no mood to soft-pedal our condition today. He says to us, as he did to those Jews who believed in him, "If you continue in my word, you are truly my disciples; and you will know the truth, and the truth will make you free."

And we are left to decide if we are going to admit our own slavery or not.

St. Augustine, in reflecting on this passage, said, "Our freedom comes when we subject ourselves to the truth." Think about that.

What does that mean?—to *subject ourselves to the truth*.

I suppose it could simply mean that we finally admit to ourselves what is true about us—that though we are created by God, in God's image, and beautiful and mysterious and wonderful in many ways, we are also broken in many ways. We are broken in body, soul, and mind. We are broken as families and communities. We are broken in our relationship with God.

It could mean admitting all that to ourselves, and that might be a start.

But to subject ourselves to *the truth* . . . is more profound than simply admitting who we really are—it is subjecting ourselves to the One who *is* the Truth, in addition to being the Way, and the Life.

The truth about us—our brokenness—does not free us. Christ does that.

For Christ, on the cross, took the truth about us and laid it upon himself. As Paul said, "For our sake [God] made him to be sin who knew no sin, so that in him we might become the righteousness of God." We might become the *righteousness of God!*

This is the truth that frees us. Or as Paul writes in our second reading for today, "There is no distinction, since *all* have sinned and fall short of the glory of God; they are now justified *by his grace as a gift,* through the redemption that is in Christ Jesus."

These are all theological ways of stating the truth that you and I are captive to sin—we are powerless against it—and God has seen that and sent Christ to set us free from this captivity.

Have you been enslaved? Yes. Are you now set free? Yes, by the grace of God, you are.

"So what does freedom in Christ look like in everyday life?" we might ask.

To answer this question, it might be best just to tell a story. This is a story told by the German theologian, Ernst Kasemann:

It seems that there was a time back in the 1950s when the country of Holland suffered many storms and floods. One of the little villages that was most affected by these storms was one of those pious places where the people felt themselves strictly bound to obey God's commandments and therefore to keep the Sabbath holy. Well, it turned out that the dike near the village was so threatened that it was going to be necessary to shore it up on the Sabbath if the inhabitants were to survive.

So the constable called the pastor of the church of this little village, and the church council was called together to discuss the matter. The discussion went much as you might expect it: "We live to obey God's commands, whether we live or we die. God can always quiet the wind and waves; we need to trust God." Not comfortable with where this conversation was leading, the pastor recalled how Jesus had said, "Human beings are not made for the Sabbath, but the Sabbath for human beings."

Just then a venerable old man stood up and said, "I have always been troubled, pastor, by something I have never yet ventured to say publicly. Now I must say it. I have always had the feeling that our Lord Jesus was a bit of a *liberal*."

That old man had it right. Jesus was a liberal. He was *liberated*. He lived in complete *liberty*—freedom, able to say and do *at all times* what God called him to say and do.

This is what freedom looks like! When you are free in Christ, you are free to do whatever God calls you to—all the time!

What does God call you to? That's for you to discern.

If God calls you to work a sixteen-hour day—and sometimes God does—you are free to do it. If God calls you to goof off all day and go hunting, or fishing, or shopping, or whatever with your best friends—and sometimes God does—you are free to do it.

If God calls you to come to worship, and God usually does, you are free to do it. And if God calls you to spend Sunday helping your neighbor shingle his house because there is no other time to do it and winter is coming, you are free to do that too.

If God calls you to give a speech or sit in silence, to stand up and fight or sit there and take a beating . . . if God calls you to run a race or tend to all those others who are having trouble even walking . . . whatever God calls you to, you are free to do it.

That is what freedom in Christ looks like. It looks like God's people, doing God's will, in all of its various and wonderful ways, in all of its joy and sorrow, in all of its sadness and celebration, *all the time*.

This is what it means to *continue* in the word of Christ.

And therefore this is what it means to be Christ's disciples.

And when you do these things simply because God calls you to them, you are free. You are free in Christ, which means you are free indeed.

Thanks be to God! Amen.

My hope is that by seeing this example, you can see that there are many ways a preacher may decide to go with a sermon. Good exegesis and good sermon design will uncover a number of avenues a preacher may take, but finally we, hopefully in concert with the Holy Spirit, choose which way we will go, and we use those pieces of the process that contribute most effectively to the final product. In no way can we ever hope to exhaust a text's possibilities, nor should we ever attempt to share with our listeners *everything* that we have discovered in the sermon process. As the old saying goes: "The preacher who attempts to exhaust a subject only ends up exhausting the listeners."

Sermon Example 2—A Sermon for the First Sunday in Advent: "You're Wearing That?"

This sermon is based on Matthew 24:36–44 (analysis will follow sermon). The central theme is: "To be prepared for Christ's coming we put on Christ"; and the central task is: "To exhort believers to lay aside the garments of sin and put on Christ daily."

Dear Friends in Christ,

I imagine the phrase "You're wearing *that?*" is one every guy hears at one time or another in his life. It often comes first from his mother, and I certainly can still hear my dear mother saying it: "You're wearing *that* to church? You're wearing *that* to the party? You're wearing *that* to the funeral?" "No, you're not." And then she'd march me upstairs to try again.

I also remember very well my mom saying that to my dad. He'd come downstairs wearing a tie that apparently did not go very well with the sport coat he had chosen, and my mom would send him back upstairs to try again—or in later years, she would just lay out his clothes for him. After all, he was color-blind.

Well, I too am color-blind, so guess what happens to me now and then? Yup, Ruth will just sort of look at me with that quizzical look that means, "Really Glenn? Are you sure about that?" And then I know, whatever it is I've chosen to wear, just doesn't quite pass inspection.

Of course, I've also been known to wear the right clothing but then get caught doing something that really doesn't go with that particular garment. Like, for instance, I might just arrive home from church and realize the compost needs to be taken out, and, yes, I'm wearing my Sunday suit, but hey, it needs to be done, and I'm coming in from the garage, and well, what can it hurt? Guys, you know what I mean.

I guess I've learned, and am still learning, that there is certain attire that goes with certain occasions and well, when they don't match up, it can be a problem.

In the reading from Romans 13 today, the Apostle Paul also exhorts us to pay attention to the garments we are wearing. He says, "Salvation is nearer to us now than when we became believers . . . [therefore] *lay aside [and take off]* the works of darkness and *put on* the armor of light."

And then Paul tells us which garments in particular we are to remove and which we are to put on. He says, "Let us live honorably as in the day, not in reveling and drunkenness, not in debauchery and licentiousness, not in quarreling and jealousy. Instead, *put on the Lord Jesus Christ*, and make no provision for the flesh, to gratify its desires."

Put on the Lord Jesus Christ.

Clothe yourselves with the Lord Jesus Christ.

That seems clearly to be God's word to us today. And the reason we are to do this is because "salvation is nearer to us now than when we became believers."

In other words, the day of the Lord's coming is nearer to us now than when we first believed.

I remember many years ago when I was called to do a funeral for an older gentleman who was not a member of the congregation, but his niece was. Uncle Charlie had been the concern of Diane for as long as I could remember. Uncle Charlie had once been married—briefly—and had even fathered a daughter, who lived far away, whom he almost never saw. So Diane, his niece, had taken it upon herself to care for him. Diane and her family treated Uncle Charlie like another grandpa. They invited him to Thanksgiving and Christmas, graduation parties, and birthday parties; now and then Diane would bring Uncle Charlie a dozen fresh cookies or a loaf of banana bread. Uncle Charlie didn't have much. He lived in a small trailer on the edge of town, pretty much kept to himself, and lived on the small pension he had gotten from working on the railroad in his younger days.

Well, when Uncle Charlie died, Diane told me all about him and asked me if I would have the service. One thing Diane mentioned was that she was buying Uncle Charlie *a new flannel shirt* to be buried in, and she'd be going down to Penney's to pick it up that afternoon. She said, "You know, Uncle Charlie didn't even own a suit, and besides his favorite outfit was a flannel shirt."

So imagine my surprise when I arrived at the funeral home on the day of the service and there was Uncle Charlie in the casket in a suit and tie. After the service I asked Diane what happened to the flannel shirt. "Oh . . . his daughter showed up, and after I'd done all the arrangements, well . . . she insisted that it wasn't proper that her dad be buried in a flannel shirt, so she went out and bought this suit. What could I do?"

I asked her, "So what did you do with the flannel shirt?" "Oh I took it back to Penney's and when they asked what the reason for the return was, I just said, 'He didn't care for the color.'"

Salvation is nearer to us than when we first became believers. That's so, isn't it? Our final breath is closer to us now than it was when we woke up today. It's the nature of things.

Jesus tells us today that we know neither the day nor the hour of the coming of the Son of Man. That's certainly true. And it is also true that we know neither the day nor the hour of our last breath. And who knows, maybe they are, in fact, one and the same. Maybe, just maybe the day of the Lord's coming is different for each one of us, and it coincides with the day of our death. I don't know.

I do know that death feels a lot like what Jesus describes in the reading today. One day the person is sitting beside you in church or across the kitchen table from you or is sleeping next to you, and the next day he or she is not. One day, you are working alongside someone and the next day you are not.

I remember Bob, a mail carrier I once knew. He was looking forward to his summer vacation. He had two weeks off. On the first day of his vacation he had a sharp pain in his side and went to the doctor to see what it was. They did some tests on him and discovered his body was filled with cancer. He died before his two-week vacation was over.

One is taken, one is left.

"You must be ready," says Jesus, "for the Son of Man is coming at an unexpected hour."

Yeah, that's true. The Son of Man *is* coming, the day of salvation *is* coming, our final day *is* coming, and Jesus says we need to be ready.

But that's the trouble—we wonder if there is *any way we can be ready*. And we are afraid we aren't.

But that's where Christ's work comes in. In the book of Galatians, Paul tells us: For "as many of you as were *baptized* into Christ have *clothed yourselves* with Christ."

God comes to us first, to make us ready.

In the water and Word, God gives us a new garment that covers our sins, and makes us new, not only on the outside, but on the inside as well. Again, as Paul says, "If anyone is in Christ, there is a new creation; everything old has passed away; everything has become new."

So, *God* makes the first move to change our wardrobe, clothing us with Christ's righteousness for the first time in our baptism.

And then each day of our lives, we are exhorted to *keep putting on Christ*, again and again. Keep putting on Christ.

We are encouraged each day to go to the closet of God's Spirit and clothe ourselves with the Spirit of Christ. And what does this look like? Paul helps us again, by sharing with us these words to the Colossians: "As God's chosen ones, holy and beloved, [you see, we are already announced chosen, holy, and beloved by virtue of our baptism into Christ!] *clothe yourselves* with compassion, kindness, humility, meekness, and patience. Bear with one another and, if anyone has a complaint against another, forgive each other; just as the Lord has forgiven you, so you also must forgive. Above all, *clothe yourselves* with love, which binds everything together in perfect harmony."

This is the wardrobe of Christ's Spirit. This is the clothing God calls you to put on every day. Just think how good you will look in compassion, kindness, humility, meekness, and patience. Everyone looks *stunning* in those garments. And how about forbearance, forgiveness, and love? Don't they look good on you? Of course they do.

And I tell you, when you put on these garments day after day, after day, you will be ready for the coming of Christ.

It turns out that living out our lives as the new creation we are in Christ is the only way to be ready to live in the new kingdom that Christ is ushering in. He wants us to practice, you see, so that when that day comes, we already know how to live in the new kingdom.

Have you ever been to a Christian funeral? Many of you have. Think about one act that is often performed: the draping of the casket with the pall. The pall is the cloth that the pallbearers place over the casket of the deceased to remind us all that God, in mercy, has *clothed us* in Christ.

And as we place the pall we say these words: "All who are baptized into Christ have *put on* Christ. In his baptism Uncle Charlie (and Aunt Betty and all of God's children) were *clothed* with Christ. In the day of Christ's coming, they shall be *clothed with glory.*"

What are you going to be wearing when Christ comes? You'll be wearing Christ, of course. Nothing could be better than that. And you are going to look fabulous! Amen.

How Does the Word Function?

This passage from Matthew 24 is the gospel lesson appointed for the First Sunday in Advent in the year of Matthew. It is the perfect text to begin the church year and the season of Advent since its clear message is: "Be prepared for the advent of our God!" So too with the epistle lesson appointed for the day, Romans 13:11–14, where the apostle exhorts us to wake from sleep, "for salvation is nearer to us now than when we became believers." Finally, Isaiah the prophet, in the first lesson, announces that because the day when God "shall judge between the nations, and shall arbitrate for many peoples" is coming, we need to "walk in the light of the Lord!"(Isa 2:1–5). It is clear that the Word is functioning in these texts to exhort, to warn, and to encourage all believers to be prepared for the coming of the Lord.

How Does the Word Not Function?

The primary message of these texts is neither law nor gospel, but rather it is what I have termed "the call to obedience."[16] It is a call to live the life that Christ frees us to live by virtue of his death and resurrection. Having said this, we note that there is more than a hint of our need for Christ in these texts. The letter to the Romans talks about the works of darkness (drunkenness, debauchery, licentiousness, quarreling, and jealousy); Isaiah reminds us that there are weapons of war that will be fashioned into plowshares and pruning hooks; and Matthew recalls the days of Noah when "the flood came and swept them all away," yet it is fair to say that this word is not explicitly a word of judgment. In other words, the function of the Word in these texts is not to condemn, and the word of the gospel (God's work of salvation) does not seem to be present at all.

With all this in mind, perhaps it is clear why I began with Paul's image of clothing in the Romans text. He exhorts us to "put on Christ," and so in very explicit terms I begin the sermon by doing exactly that. My next move is the hint of the law described above, but I do it by shining the light brightly on that portion of the Romans text that says "salvation is nearer to us now than when we became believers." This is done to ensure that the listeners make a clear connection between the need to be prepared and their own mortality. I decided that the call to watch and be prepared would

16. Note: Some theologians have named this call to obedience the "second use of the gospel." This is a way to distinguish it from the so-called "third use of the law," with which Lutherans struggle.

fall on deaf ears if the law was only heard as the seemingly distant threat of judgment, not one that is well known to us all, namely that today could be our last day.

A Strategy for Adding Law and Gospel

The gospel move needed to be done with texts outside the appointed lessons, so the passage from Galatians begins it where I remind the listeners that "as many of you as were baptized into Christ have clothed yourselves with Christ," thereby making the connection between the exhortation to put on Christ and Paul's announcement that in baptism we receive our first wardrobe change. From there I go on to quote further from Paul's letters reminding the listeners that "if anyone is in Christ, there is a new creation" (2 Cor 5:17). Eventually I return to Paul's words in the Romans 13 text that began the sermon and then appeal to one more epistle, by using the words of Paul from Colossians 3 where he exhorts us to put on the clothing of compassion, kindness, humility, and so forth. In so doing I return to the primary message of the day, which is the call to obedience to "put on Christ," but I do so by anchoring that obedience clearly in the work of Christ in baptism.

With Whom Are We Identifying in the Text?

It is always tempting for us to assume that a text is speaking to everyone but the preacher. These texts are no different. We might look at these texts and conclude, "Jesus is right. *My folks* are not prepared! I need to tell them to get their act together!" That would be an exhortation, of course, but the mistake in this course of action is that we have once again identified ourselves with *Jesus*. We have assumed that this word is not spoken first to us! No, as always, we must not identify with Jesus; we must identify with those to whom Jesus is speaking, and so in these texts we must identify with those unprepared for the advent of our God.

In the introductory scene, I am attempting to identify clearly with one who is not clothed rightly. In a humorous fashion I am saying, "Look, I know what it's like to be dressed inappropriately," and then I continue through the sermon to identify myself with the unprepared even saying at the midpoint, "But that's the trouble—we wonder if there is any way we can be ready. And we are afraid we aren't." Notice the use of the pronoun "we." I believe it is always very important for us to identify with our listeners as one to whom the word is being spoken.

The Law/Gospel Couplet

I imagine there are many couplets that might work for this particular sermon but the one that I chose was anxiety/certitude. It seemed to me in studying these texts that the law functions primarily to increase anxiety, continually pushing the question: "Are you ready for the advent of Christ?" In the middle of the sermon, as I've pointed out above, I even say, "We wonder if there is any way we can be ready. And we are afraid we aren't."

The gospel half of the couplet then must function to provide certitude, which is exactly what I attempt to do by calling on the Galatians passage to announce the good word that "all who have been baptized into Christ have put on Christ." It is the announcement of God's action to ready us for Christ's coming. I want to say clearly, "You *are* ready for Christ's coming, because *God* has made you ready." In this move I am attempting to move the listener towards faith in God's action and away from the anxiety that results in believing that it is only *our* action that makes us ready for the coming of Christ.

Exegetical Work

I often begin my exegetical work by being sure that I understand the context of the passages, and today's sermon is no different. Since I will be centering the sermon on the gospel lesson and the

Roman's passage, I spend most of my time looking at these texts. I note that the Matthew text is part of a larger end-of-time discourse that encompasses all of Matthew 24 and 25. Seeing this I am drawn to one key word that is integral to this kind of discourse, the word *parousia*. Parousia is often translated "advent" or "coming," but it is clearly a particular kind of event associated with the arrival of a ruler among the people. This is pointed out in a helpful article in Kittel's dictionary: "The customary honours of the parousia of a ruler are: flattering addresses, tributes, delicacies, asses to ride on and for baggage, improvement of streets, golden wreaths or money, and feeding of the sacred crocodiles."[17]

Clearly then, the parousia of Christ about which Matthew speaks is not simply Christ's coming, in the sense of a person coming to visit, but his coming is an event for which one is necessarily *very* prepared.

In the Romans text, I am also drawn to one key Greek word, which catches my attention during my translation of this text. That word is *kairos*, often simply translated as "time." Again Kittel is helpful in making clear the difference between kairos time and regular time (chronos time). In the article in Kittel's dictionary we learn that kairos is a "decisive moment" or a "fateful and decisive point, ordained by God." It is sometimes called the "time of judgment" and in all cases it is a time that no one may ignore.[18]

This idea, that the time about which Paul and Matthew speak is not a time we may ignore, is also then an idea that helps shape the sermon, giving urgency to this message.

In addition to this translation work and work in theological dictionaries, I am also instructed by the words of Luther in his "Lectures on Romans" where he writes about "Christians who are living lukewarm lives and are snoring in their smugness"[19] and by the commentary of Paul Achtemeier who writes that "Christians . . . in Paul's view, are creatures of the future, not the past. . . . Liberated from the burdens of a sinful past, the Christian

17. Kittel, *TDNT*, 5:860.
18. Kittel, *TDNT*, 3:455–59.
19. Oswald, "Lectures on Romans," 478.

strides with confident step into the future."[20] These and additional words of wisdom from online commentaries are always helpful in doing this exegetical work.[21]

The Crossings Method

In looking at the archived examples on the Crossings Community website, I note that there are several sermon designs posted for Matthew 24:36–44 under "Year A Gospel" for the First Sunday in Advent. One example from 2011 by Paul Jaster entitled "Christ's Advent, Catastrophe Averted" is a fine example of how this method can work. His design is set up in the following way:

D1: Normally preoccupied	P6: Watchful readiness
D2: Dangerously unaware	P5: Freeing/Refreshing/ Awakening
D3: Cataclysmic catastrophe	P4: Surprising coming

What is instructive to note is that Jaster clearly has been drawn to the word in Matthew 24:38–39 translated "flood." This word in Greek is the word *kataclysmos* from which we get our word *cataclysm*. Jaster centers on the idea that an event is coming that will undo all the plans of humanity, but he makes a wonderful turn in the announcement of the gospel (in P4) when he announces that the cataclysm that changes the world is the cross of Christ.

While this design is a wonderful way to go, in my own work I was drawn to other key words and therefore did not follow this design. However I am always reminded by the Crossings Method that the pivotal point of the sermon must be anchored in the work of Christ, and so I strive for this in every sermon.

20. Achtemeier, *Romans*, 212.

21. One of the best single online resources for preachers is textweek.com where many of the known resources for any particular lectionary text are listed according to genre. This is an outstanding resource.

6

Final Thoughts

MY ONLY FEAR IN writing this book is that readers will conclude that, because I have offered here a rather methodical way of proceeding in creating a Law and Gospel sermon, somehow this sort of preaching can be reduced to a formula. Nothing could be further from the truth. Indeed I will venture to say that any preacher who adopts this method or any other and thinks that in so doing she or he will have the magic formula to sermon-writing that will guarantee a profound and moving sermon week in, week out, is guaranteed of only one thing—disappointment. The preaching of God's word is never completely under our control, nor should it be. We are certainly called to work hard at it, yet it remains, in large part, God's work, not ours.

Herman Stuempfle and others have written about the sermon being *a living entity* akin to life in the womb of a mother. I like this image. It suggests that a sermon has a life of its own, and this life is not completely our creation or the creation of our listeners, but rather the Creator is at work as well, and what finally is born when a sermon is preached is the work of all three: preacher, listener, and Creator. The sermon is like all life, then, a miracle. It emerges from the womb of the Word, made up of the preacher, the people, and God's Spirit; and it lives and breathes as it does the work of God among the people of God in God's world.

Another image that is very important in my thinking is the sermon as *a mystery* akin to the sacraments of Baptism and Holy Communion. As in the sacraments, the sermon has with it a physical element, in this case physical speech, which brings the gift of grace to God's people. Also, like the sacraments, preaching is commanded by God, and with that command comes a promise: "So faith comes from what is heard, and what is heard comes through the preaching of Christ" (Rom 10:17). As law and gospel are announced, God's grace is given and people are convicted, chastened, forgiven, instructed, and encouraged. The Word then accomplishes God's work much as the sacraments do. All are invited to hear the Word, just as all are (or, in my view, ought to be) invited to the table, for in both the Word and the sacrament, God is at work doing the saving work that is God's will for all.

I believe also that Karl Barth was right when he said that the Word longs to disclose itself. The Word of God has within it God's desire to save, and we are simply the persons who are privileged to free the Word to do its saving work. This, it seems to me, is vital for us to believe. If we believe that the Word longs to be heard, then we can be confident that as we go to our study week after week, praying for a word to bring to God's people, that God's good will is that a word *will* come; it will be born in us once again, and the miracle of the Word will come forth yet again.

What a marvelous privilege we have as preachers. We are, as the Apostle Paul says, "stewards of the mysteries of God," entrusted with something so precious as God's word, somehow declared to be fit for the job, even as we remain "foremost among sinners." I'm not sure what is more surprising—that *God's* work is done through us, or that God's work is done through *us*.

Some writers in recent times have argued that God's people are no longer served very well by having one person stand up among the many and speak a word. They have said that the day is long past when one person's voice is sufficient for this task, and we ought to sit down and allow the people of God to speak the Word to one another. There is wisdom in this argument, of course, for undoubtedly some of us have misused our office of preaching in ways that have not been life-giving to God's people. Yet, I continue to believe that God's people are served well by preaching that both boldly proclaims the reign of God among us and modestly accepts the limitations of that proclamation. I do not, for a moment, believe that my word on Sunday morning is the last word on any subject, or that somehow I am indispensable to God's work in the world. I do, however, believe that the sermon, though only a fleeting moment in history, lasting no longer than the breath required to send the words out into the air, is *an important moment* in the ongoing conversation of God with God's people. After all, what is life, but a series of moments, and who is to say which of those might be life changing?

I close with an image that remains dear to me. It was written by that courageous and undaunted preacher of God's word, Dietrich Bonhoeffer, who endured so much yet continued to preach God's word, confident that God's work was being done through him. He wrote:

> The proclaimed word is the Christ bearing human nature. This word is no new incarnation, but the Incarnate One who bears the sins of the world. Through the Holy Spirit this word becomes the actualization of his acceptance and sustenance. The word of the sermon intends to accept humanity, nothing else. It wants to bear the whole of human nature. In the congregation all sins should be cast upon the Word. Preaching must be so done that the hearer places all his [sic] needs, cares, fears, and sins upon the Word. The Word accepts these things. When preaching is done in this way, it is the proclamation of Christ. This proclamation of Christ does not regard its primary responsibility to be giving advice, arousing emotions, or stimulating the will—it will do these things, too—but its intention is to sustain us. The Word is there that burdens might be laid upon it. We are all borne up by the word of Christ.[1]

Imagine that! We are called to free Christ to rise again and walk among God's people as the Word. And this Word bears all

1. Bonhoeffer, *Worldly Preaching*, 102.

the sins and burdens of God's people. Could anything be a greater calling or mystery than that!

Soli Deo Gloria!

Appendix

A Worksheet for Sermon Design

1. How does the Word function in the text?
What is God saying/doing? What is Jesus saying/doing? What is the Spirit saying/doing? What is the prophet/writer/speaker accomplishing within this text?

2. How is the Word *not* functioning in the text?
Is there no law in this text—no word that exposes our need for Christ? Or is there no gospel in this text—no word that proclaims what God has done in Christ? Or is there no call to obedience in this text—no word that instructs how one is invited to live in response to the gospel?

3. With whom are you identifying in the text?
Remember: It is important always to identify with the people who are addressed by the Word, not with Jesus or God or the Word itself.

4. What, if any, call to obedience is there in this text? What, in the text, functions to invite us to live in response to God's work?

5. What law/gospel couplet is suggested by this text? (See Stuemp-fle's and Lischer's examples in chapter 3 or come up with your own couplet.)

6. Exegetical work: What does translation work open up for you in this text? What do you gain from reading different translations of this text or from reading this text aloud or in the first person from the perspective of different characters? What insights do you gain through word studies or lexical work? What commentary work or work within an active text study helps you hear this text afresh? Are there online resources that can open up this text to you? How about rhetorical analysis or narrative analysis—do they help you in gaining insight into this text?

7. How does the Crossings Method work with this text? How does the diagnosis/prognosis structure help you design a sermon based on this text?

8. Consider the insights of the pioneers of the New Homiletic.

- Craddock: How are you bringing the experience of the text to the listener, not just the content?

- Rice: How are you helping listeners recognize their shared story in this text?

- Lowry: How are you moving your listeners from disequilibrium to equilibrium?

- Buttrick: How many moves have you made in the sermon design? Too many or too few?

- Mitchell: Where is celebration evident in your design and how much do you celebrate?

Bibliography

Achtemeier, Paul J. *Romans*. Interpretation commentary series. Atlanta: John Knox, 1985.

Allen, O. Wesley, Jr., ed. *The Renewed Homiletic*. Minneapolis: Fortress, 2010.

Bachmann, E. Theodore, ed. "How the Christian Should Regard Moses." In *Word and Sacrament I*, 155–74. Luther's Works 35. Philadelphia: Muhlenberg, 1960.

Barth, Karl. *Homiletics*. Louisville: Westminster John Knox, 1991.

Black, Kathy. *A Healing Homiletic: Preaching and Disability*. Nashville: Abingdon, 1996.

Bonhoeffer, Dietrich. *Worldly Preaching: Lectures on Homiletics*. New York: Crossroad, 1991.

Braaten, Carl E. *Principles of Lutheran Theology*. Philadelphia: Fortress, 1983.

Brown, Raymond E. *The Gospel according to John I–XII*. Anchor Bible 29. New York: Doubleday, 1966.

Buttrick, David. *Homiletic: Moves and Structures*. Philadelphia: Fortress, 1987.

Cary, Phillip. "The Lutheran Codicil: From Augustine's Grace to Luther's Gospel." *Logia: A Journal of Lutheran Theology* 20 (2011) 5.

Childers, Jana. *Performing the Word: Preaching as Theatre*. Nashville: Abingdon, 1998.

Craddock, Fred B. *As One Without Authority*. 4th ed. St. Louis: Chalice, 2001.

———. *Preaching*. Nashville: Abingdon, 1985.

Ebeling, Gerhard. *Luther: An Introduction to His Thought*. Philadelphia: Fortress, 1972.

Forde, Gerhard O. *The Law Gospel Debate*. Minneapolis: Augsburg, 1969.

———. *Theology Is for Proclamation*. Minneapolis: Fortress, 1990.

George, Timothy, ed. *Reformation Commentary on Scripture*. 13 vols. (projected). Downers Grove: IVP Academic, 2012–.

Hall, Thor. *The Future Shape of Preaching*. Philadelphia: Fortress, 1971.

Kittel, Gerhard. *Theological Dictionary of the New Testament*. Grand Rapids: Eerdmans, 1964.

Kolb, Robert, and Timothy W. Wengert, eds. *The Book of Concord*. Minneapolis: Fortress, 2000.

Lischer, Richard. *A Theology of Preaching*. Nashville: Abingdon, 1981.

Long, Thomas G. *Preaching and Literary Forms of the Bible*. Philadelphia: Fortress, 1989.

Lose, David. *Confessing Jesus Christ: Preaching in a Post-Modern World*. Grand Rapids: Eerdmans, 2003.

Lowry, Eugene L. *The Homiletical Plot*. Atlanta: John Knox, 1978.

———. *The Sermon: Dancing the Edge of Mystery*. Nashville: Abingdon, 1997.

Malysz, Piotr J. "Third Use of the Law: Freedom and Obedience in Christian Life." Chapter 7 in *Preaching and Teaching the Law and Gospel of God*, edited by Carl E. Braaten. Minneapolis: American Lutheran Publicity Bureau, 2013.

Mitchell, Henry. *Celebration and Experience in Preaching*. Nashville: Abingdon, 1990.

Monson, Glenn L. "A Funny Thing Happened on the Way through the Sermon." *Dialog: A Journal of Theology* 43 (2004) 304–11.

Oden, Thomas C., ed. *Ancient Christian Commentary on Scripture*. 12 vols. Downers Grove: InterVarsity, 2003.

Ong, Walter J. *Orality and Literacy: The Technologizing of the Word*. London: Routledge, 1982.

———. *The Presence of the Word*. Minneapolis: University of Minnesota Press, 1967.

Oswald, Hilton C., ed. *Lectures on Romans*. Luther's Works 25. St. Louis: Concordia, 1972.

Pelikan, Jaroslav, ed. *Sermons on the Gospel of St. John*. Chaps. 6–8. Luther's Works 23. St. Louis: Concordia, 1959.

———. *Lectures on Galatians* (1535). Luther's Works 26. St. Louis: Concordia, 1963.

Powell, Mark Allan. *What Is Narrative Criticism?* Minneapolis: Augsburg Fortress, 1990.

Reid, Robert Stephen. "Faithful Preaching: Preaching Epistemes, Faith Stages, and Rhetorical Practice." *Journal of Communication and Religion* 21 (1998) 169.

Roth, Robert Paul. *Story and Reality: An Essay on Truth*. Grand Rapids: Eerdmans, 1973.

Schlafer, David J. *Your Way with God's Word: Discovering Your Distinctive Preaching Voice*. Boston: Cowley, 1995.

Steimle, Edmund A., et al. *Preaching the Story*. Philadelphia: Fortress, 1980.

Stuempfle, Herman G., Jr. *Preaching Law and Gospel*. Philadelphia: Fortress, 1978.

Taylor, Barbara Brown. *The Preaching Life*. Boston: Cowley, 1993.

Troeger, Thomas H. *Imagining a Sermon*. Nashville: Abingdon, 1990.

———. *Ten Strategies for Preaching in a Multi-Media Culture*. Nashville: Abingdon, 1996.

Wilson, Paul Scott. *Preaching and Homiletical Theory*. St. Louis: Chalice, 2004.

Zahrnt, Heinz. *The Question of God*. New York: Harcourt Brace Jovanovich, 1969.

Scriptures Index

99

44250313R00068

Made in the USA
San Bernardino, CA
10 January 2017